Storyteller

Storyteller

**Writing Lessons and More
from 27 Years of the
Clarion Writers' Workshop**

» Kate Wilhelm

Small Beer Press
Northampton, MA

Small Beer Press
176 Prospect Avenue
Northampton, MA 01060
www.smallbeerpress.com
info@smallbeerpress.com

www.katewilhelm.com

Distributed to the trade by Consortium.

Library of Congress Cataloging-in-Publication Data

Wilhelm, Kate.
  Storyteller : writing lessons and more from 27 years of the clarion writers' workshop / by Kate Wilhelm.
      p. cm.
  Includes index.
  ISBN 1-931520-16-X (alk. paper)
  1. English language--Rhetoric--Study and teaching--United States 2. Creative writing--Study and teaching--United States. 3. Wilhelm, Kate. I. Title.

PE1405.U6W55 2005
808'.042'071073--dc22

                                                        2005013481

ISBN 13: 978-1-931520-16-4
ISBN 10: 1-931520-16-X

          2 3 4 5 6 7 8 9 0

Printed on 50# Natures Natural recycled paper by Thomson-Shore in Dexter, MI. Text set in Centaur 12. Titles in Arial Black.

Cover illustration © CORBIS

Contents

Dedicated to the memory of Damon Knight,
Leonard Isaacs, and R. Glenn Wright.

» Preface

This book is not really a memoir, not a tour through my personal life, my traumas and triumphs. It isn't really a history or a how-to-write book, although I do go into detail about many of the lectures and exercises that Damon and I formulated over the years. It is an account of my years spent in lecturing and teaching at the Clarion Science Fiction and Fantasy Workshop. It is how I remember Clarion, which Lucius Shepard aptly called a boot camp for writers.

The first half of the book is concerned with the beginnings, the facilities, the students who made up the attendees, part of the staff that made it all possible. The second half concerns the stories we workshopped and the lessons and exercises we developed from them. Some of the lessons were mostly Damon's, some mostly mine, but finally all of them were jointly ours. I don't use any actual manuscripts, just my memories of the stories, and the notes I made at the time.

This is not so much how to write as how *not* to write, because that is what we concerned ourselves with most of the time. We repeatedly saw the same problems and tried to address *why* they were problems and possible ways of correcting them.

Damon Knight and I were associated with Clarion from its inception in 1967 through the year 1994. Following Damon's death in 2002, I came to realize I was the only one remaining who was there from the start, and I yielded to the impulse to record my memories of Clarion, what it meant to us, and what it means today.

I am grateful to many people for their support and help in gathering the dates and facts from years gone by—Tess Tavormina, Mary Sheridan, and Lister Matheson have been unstinting in giving time and information. Herman and Alice King were especially gracious with their own recollections. Any dates, facts, or details that are wrong are solely my own responsibility.

Thanks also to Vonda N. McIntyre (vondanmcintyre.com) for her generous input in relating how Clarion West was started, and how it continues. It should be noted that for information concerning either Clarion Workshop, the following addresses are helpful, especially for those former students who have lost touch or are among the missing in the alumni lists: clarionwest.org and clarion@msu.edu.

Michigan State University was invaluable as the host for so many years to the workshop. And Lymann Briggs College was always supportive as the sponsor for the workshop. Special thanks here to Dr. Edward Ingraham, Director of the Lyman Briggs School, for his support and friendship through the years. And finally, many thanks to Robin Scott Wilson, who started it all, and continues today as a strong advocate for the workshop.

All these people played a role. Without any one of them the outcome might have been quite different. The workshop has been and still is a tremendous influence on the writers involved, and on the writing community as a whole. This book is how I remember Clarion.

In the Beginning

To understand Clarion, you must first know something about the Milford Conference. It was a workshop started by Judith Merril, James Blish, and Damon Knight in the mid-1950s, with the idea that professional writers would benefit from, and enjoy, getting together to critique one another's work and talk shop. It was set up for eight days, with critique sessions daily from about noon until late afternoon, dinner, and then discussions that often lasted until dawn. It was enormously successful from the start, attracting luminaries in the science fiction field from all over the country and England. Those who attended the full eight days over the years included Judith Merril, editor of the prestigious *Year's Best Science Fiction* series, James Blish and Damon Knight, both award-winning critics and editors, Ben Bova, Harlan Ellison, Piers Anthony, John Brunner, Anne McCaffrey, Carol Emshwiller, Algis Budrys, and Richard McKenna.

Among those who came only for a weekend were Brian Aldiss, Arthur C. Clarke, Isaac Asimov, Robert Silverberg, Fred Pohl, and Theodore Sturgeon. Altogether it was an inspiring and sometimes intimidating group.

I was invited to attend my first Milford conference in 1959, and I remember it as vividly as if it had happened only a year or two ago. I was terrified, for one thing, and justifiably so. I was as green as any novice writer who ever dreamed of becoming a professional. I knew nothing about critiquing, or accepting criticism, and my story took a drubbing that no Clarion student could ever equal. Afterward, I put on my brightest lipstick and went to the riverbank on the Delaware River and threw stones into the water as hard as I could, muttering, "I'll show you, James Blish. I'll show you, Damon Knight. I'll show you..." I don't remember how far I got before my arm got tired.

Later, I realized that another beginning writer who had also attended for the first time received hardly any criticism, yet I knew his story had been as bad as or worse than mine. And I had to admit I deserved every word of criticism directed at me, and furthermore that I needed it, and that the professional writers had taken me seriously.

That was a big discovery: other writers had treated me and my work seriously in a way no one had done previously. I had been writing and publishing stories for three years at that time, and I was clueless about why some of them were accepted and others had not been. The Milford Conference was my own personal boot camp.

I had not realized until that week how starved I was for any intellectual stimulation, real conversation about writing, ideas, philosophy, theology, politics, everything. My adrenaline was so charged that for the entire week, I found I could not sleep. When I boarded my plane to head back home to Louisville, the flight attendant suggested I pretend to be asleep when we landed in Washington because someone might be bumped for another passenger, and they were always reluctant to awaken a sleeping passenger. I settled into my seat, and the next thing I knew someone was shaking my arm to say we were in Louisville. I suppose the attendant thought I was the best pretender she had ever encountered. It was the only time in my life I ever slept on an airplane.

Four years later, Damon and I, both divorced from previous

spouses, were married. That year, because of the pressure of other work, Jim Blish and Judy Merril had to drop out of the arduous task of organizing the conference, although they both attended regularly, and Damon, with whatever help I could provide, ran the conference from then on. The Milford Conference, which had introduced us, became our first team effort.

Those who attended for the whole of the workshop brought several copies of one short story, which everyone read when they could find time. The protocol of the workshop was to arrange the furniture in more or less a circle, begin the critique at one side of the writer whose work was being discussed and continue around the circle until everyone had spoken. Then the writer, who had been silent, could express gratitude, explain, defend, lash out in anger, cringe in silence, laugh or weep. We saw all these reactions at one time or another.

In 1966, Judy Merril and I put together a petition protesting the Vietnam War and circulated it for signatures among the professional writers in the science fiction field and then published it. The following year Robin Scott Wilson attended the Milford Conference. It was no secret that Robin had been in the CIA before turning to teaching and writing, but paranoia was running high, and Judy and I were concerned that perhaps he had not dropped the CIA altogether, that perhaps our protest had drawn attention, possibly we were on a list, being checked out. It did nothing to ease our apprehension when at every turn we caught glimpses of Robin asking questions and taking notes.

On the final day of the workshop, Robin explained his motives. He was teaching at Clarion State College, he said, and he was planning on doing a summer workshop in creative writing. After observing the Milford Conference for a week, he intended to model his workshop on the Milford method. At that time he asked four people to come as visiting lecturers. He said funding would not cover more than four, and they would be paid a pittance. He planned to do the first and last week himself. The four he had chosen were Damon Knight, Judy Merril, Fritz Leiber, and Harlan Ellison. Damon told him that if he went, I would have to go also, and Robin, always the perfect gentleman, blinked and said, "Well, of course."

That summer of 1968, my two older sons were with their father, Damon's three children were with their mother in Port Jervis, New York, and we took our two-year-old, Jonathan, across the state from Milford to Clarion, Pennsylvania.

We arrived hot and tired from the long drive, so our own condition was not surprising, but we were surprised to find Robin worn to a nub, the students in a final stage of meltdown, exhausted, bored, hungry, and with so much tension running through all of them, they crackled.

Clarion in the sixties was a town out of a Jack Finney novel, a town that to all appearances had not moved in time since the late thirties. Everything closed at dusk and nothing opened on Sunday. If you ran out of gas on the weekend, you had to wait until Monday to refuel. The single movie theater had one movie for the entire summer, *Attack of the Killer Tomatoes!*, I think it was. Although that might have been the following year. There were no bookstores, but it is likely that when the college was holding regular sessions, there might have been one. No recreation facilities. The swimming pool had been closed for repairs a year or so earlier. There were few outlets for the students' tension. For a break in the monotony, some of the students went to stand on the corner of the main street and watch cars go by, now and then leaning over to peer inside. The hostility between town and gown was never higher. Some of the town boys caught one of the students, a hippie-freak-pinko-commie type, no doubt, and cut his hair. Long hair on males was a no-no. And quite a few of our men had long hair, including Damon.

The college cafeteria food was atrocious, and there were two restaurants in town that were not much better. At the restaurant called the best, I asked what the stuffed shrimp was stuffed with, and the waitress shook her head and said, "I don't know, but I wouldn't eat it." No one in our group did, either.

We were housed, students and visiting lecturers alike, in a charming old building that had been condemned some time in the past. There was a lot of mellow yellow brickwork, arched windows and doors, wide corridors with old-fashioned linoleum on the floors. A wide porch contained a few chairs. One expected to see a swing, but no. A double-door entrance opened into a large lounge, with halls leading off in two directions. Typewriters were set up in the lounge. The men's dorm rooms were on the second floor, the women's on the ground floor. I was an added complication; it had been decided that it would be highly improper to house me near the men, and Damon could not be housed in the wing with the women. We had our room on the first floor, the only occupants of one entire wing. Damon, of course, had to stay out of the other wing altogether. He could enter the lounge and go to our room, or go up to the next level, where I was forbidden.

Over the weekend, Robin's wife, Pat, arranged a babysitter for me so that I could attend the regular workshop sessions. I don't know if Robin anticipated that, but no question was raised and I was accepted. And that made us twenty-eight in all: twenty-five students and three professionals. It was no wonder the group was grim and somewhat apprehensive. No doubt the students felt they had been browbeaten thoroughly by the professional writer-lecturers who had come before us, and we were going to add to their misery. I could well understand their apprehension, having suffered from it so recently, but, still, Damon and I were dismayed to see so much unhappiness.

With such a large group, the critique session were grueling, and took a very long time to get through, even though many of the students had very little to say about any one story. After three or four hours, everyone was exhausted. That was not good considering that it was only Monday, and we had two more weeks to go.

After that first workshop on Monday, Damon and I took time out and went to town to find a ten-cent store where we bought superballs, water guns, and balloons, a lot of them. And that afternoon we had a grand melee on the porch and in the shrubs around it. Everyone got soaked. When the water fights spread into the lounge and papers were getting wet, I took a stand by the door and refused to admit any combatants. I declared a rule that quickly became a general rule: no water guns were allowed where manuscripts were present or typewriters set up. That meant no gunfights in the lounge, but it didn't matter; there was a lot of space outside. And the warriors needed a haven where they could catch their breath now and then. And reload.

The ground beneath the shrubbery became so saturated with superballs that when one was lost, two different ones were found.

After that, things got much, much better. It was if the students had been in a pressure cooker for four weeks and someone had opened a valve to relieve the pressure before it erupted. I suspect it did them a world of good to be able to turn on the authority of the week and let him or them have it.

The workshop schedule appeared to be reasonably undemanding: from nine until noon or one o'clock there was the circle of students critiquing four or five stories in the Milford method. Each student was required to say something, then the visiting writer spoke, and finally Robin. For the rest of the day, all evening and early morning, they were free to write and read. There was always a group that hung out around us, as I imagined they had done with the other writers. They just wanted to be nearby, talk or not, ask questions or not, always ready to latch on to any word we uttered.

Most of them managed to write at least one story a week. The stories were Xeroxed and made available to be read. The first year, there were never enough copies to go around; some vanished, some went to dorm rooms and stayed for many hours, and as a result, often students were up until nearly dawn trying to catch up. Now and then they simply failed to find a manuscript. In subsequent years, each student and the instructors were given a copy of everything, an enormous increase in expense, but a necessary one. As it turned out, there was very little free time. For many of the students, it was the first time they had ever been in a group of like-minded people where they could talk about anything and everything and not be guarded, or feel the need to explain everything they said. That was liberating and time consuming. The conversations were incessant.

After his daily nap, I took Jonathan for a walk in his stroller, and usually some of the students came with us and we talked. I realized early on that the women were anxious to learn how a woman writer coped with family and a career. When I told them that there were five more children who were with us most of the time, they were amazed, disbelieving, aghast—all the above. I think it was a good thing that the students saw that it was possible. Not easy, but possible.

One of the male students had not written a word during the

first four weeks, and we drew him aside to try to find out why. He confessed that his mother had written his submission story. Damon and I were flabbergasted. We didn't know quite what to do about that. Finally I said, "Well, you're here, she isn't. And you have to write a story before you leave."

He wrote one. It was ghastly, but it was a story, and he wrote it himself.

Another student turned in a story that was clearly a rewrite of one of my own stories. Again, we felt helpless, and this time we turned to Robin. He read both stories and agreed that it was as near plagiarism as one could get without using a Xerox machine. He took that student aside and lectured him on the penalty for plagiarism, and we moved on. A day or two later, we addressed the subject of plagiarism in class.

Toward the end of our week, Damon and I talked about what we had not accomplished, and what we had hoped to get done. Then we asked Robin if we could stay for the sixth and final week. He explained again that he had no funding for it, and we said that was fine if we could keep our room, and we offered to pay for our meals. We all knew that was the final sacrifice, to pay for that wretched food. Damon said it was the first time he realized that a determined cook could ruin a grilled cheese sandwich. Anyway, Robin agreed, and we did stay for the sixth week, but we didn't have to pay for our meals.

One of the reasons we wanted to stay on was that we had come to learn that a literary or academic approach to story is not the same as a writer's analytical approach. Robin is a wonderful teacher; he knows a participle from a gerund and can explain the difference with aplomb. He got the workshop off to a fine start by teaching the students the tools they would need for the weeks to follow, the language to express their critiques, and how the workshop would function. He made it clear that there would be no *ad hominem* criticism. Only the written work could be criticized or praised, never the writer.

Robin's finesse at organizing and managing events is unmatchable. He can analyze a story to the nth degree, but his approach was often that of a literary critic assessing a finished piece of work. For example, he looked for and explicated theme and symbolism, and most writers seldom think of either when they are writing or critiquing.

We saw the stories as works in progress and were more interested in how each story was made, how the parts worked, if they fit together, and how to make the story better. Or if it didn't work as story, find out why and try to find a way to make it work. All too often there was no way to fix it. Damon always read with a pencil in his hand, editing as he went; I couldn't do that.

I had to read everything twice, first to see if it was a horse, then to determine if it had four legs, a head, and the other necessary parts. Only after that could I look at the actual prose. It was time-consuming and laborious work for both of us, usually done late at night after we chased away the students.

As for symbolism, I tried very hard to avoid mentioning it at all. Symbols are so intimately bound to the writer's personal experiences and style, that to draw attention to them might cause the writer to become self-conscious, and even to try to impose symbols, instead of letting them emerge naturally. A writer friend announced one year at Milford that she had come to realize how much she was trying to manipulate symbols, insert them at every opportunity, and only afterward recognized how false they all were, how contrived. She had given up the use altogether, she said firmly. The story she handed in that year was about a woman who was stuck in a relationship from which she could see no escape. The woman is seen walking in a moonlit garden where alabaster or marble statues are on display, each one icelike, frozen in time and space. But the writer swore she had given up symbols.

So our approach was analytical, not literary. We were dealing with raw material, not a finished piece of work. For many writers, no story is ever truly finished; at some point it is abandoned. It is important to learn which abandoned story should be submitted for possible publication, and which ones should be put away and chalked up as another learning experience.

We stayed on for the sixth and final week, fumbling and bumbling our way through, more often than not feeling inadequate as teachers, especially in light of Robin's erudition and training. Neither Damon nor I had had teaching experience, and we were learning by trial and error what was effective and what was not. And we were both learning how very much we did not know well enough to explain things we had taken for granted or knew through our own experience but had not articulated. We did not have a way to express the deeper knowledge all writers acquire sooner or later about technique, methodology, about craft. We were treating these beginning writers the same way the professional writers at Milford treated each other, and we both sensed that it was not appropriate, but we did not know what was needed yet.

Then it was over, and it was as if time had gone crazy. Endless days and nights that had been packed too full, stretches of boredom, terrible food, too little sleep, and—suddenly it was over. At the end, it seemed the two weeks had been impossibly swift. So much had been left undone, unsaid, unexamined, unexplained.

Robin invited us back the following year, and we were eager to try again, to do better, not to leave so many loose ends. In theory, Damon was to be there for one week, and I for one. In practice, we were both there for the last two weeks that first Clarion—and all but one that followed through 1994. In the beginning it was incidental; it was just more convenient. The final weeks worked out better for us, giving us a little time following the Milford Conference before we tackled the Clarion Workshop. The one time that we did not follow that schedule, we all agreed, was not satisfactory.

As it turned out, the last two weeks go better if there is not a change of lecturers. Each lecturer brings a valuable and unique approach, a different emphasis and perspective, and each one requires a shift in the expectations of the students. The last week is a time of consolidation, a time for the students to put to use some of the lessons learned throughout the entire first five weeks, and it is a hardship for them to be confronted with yet another different approach. We felt it was a time for them to slow down and think more cogently of the story in progress rather than rush it through before this teacher left and a new one arrived.

Also, inevitably, the last week is when students are preparing to reenter the real world of "out there." They come from many different situations, and the situations will be there when they return. One former student told me that one of the most valuable things she took home with her was my advice about time. No one gives it to a new writer, or in many cases to an established writer. Each and every one of us has to take it, forcibly if necessary, by wile, bribery, any method that works. You have to take the time, to weigh it against whatever else is happening, to give it up somewhere else, sacrifice time with other people, time for movies, time for television, fun, games, partying, sleep, or something. There is always some time every day to set aside and declare one's own, but it requires a lot of self-discipline to seize it and keep it. If not every day, then three days a week, and if that's still impossible, one day a week. It's hard in the beginning because there is no payback, no tangible reward for all that time spent alone in thought or at a keyboard, and life keeps getting in the way. But it is absolutely necessary to find the time and keep it inviolable and recognized by the private world of the writer that it is not to be invaded.

Paradoxically, and cruelly, the ones you love the most and who love you are the greatest problem. They see that you are suffering, alone, withdrawn, getting nowhere apparently, and they want to relieve you, help you, ease your pain. A movie, a game, a walk or drive, something is offered, and if you say no, feelings get hurt, guilt arises. You have to decide which guilt to live with, the guilt of denying the companionship, or the guilt of yielding and not writing or working at an aspect of writing.

Two precedents were set during that first year, one was to have two writers who stayed for the final two weeks.

The other precedent established was the acceptance that a little bit of manic insanity was a good thing. Water gun fights, water balloon ambushes, superball brawls; all good things.

Can Writing Be Taught?

Damon and I talked a lot about Clarion during the following year, and one of the questions we returned to often was simply this: Can writing be taught? There are many writers who say emphatically that the answer is no. I see their point. High school and college creative writing classes are too often a joke, taught by non-writers without a clue about the real world of publishing and what makes for a publishable story in contemporary markets. For most writers struggling alone, the learning curve from the first attempt to write to becoming an accomplished writer is very long, years in many cases. And all the while they are being taught by rejection slips, by trial and error; they are learning what works for them and what doesn't. Even after they have published a few stories, they often can't see why one story was accepted and not another.

The answer we arrived at was a qualified yes; *some* things about writing can be taught. Possibly there were shortcuts, methods to reduce that long learning period. Anyone with fair talent, a great deal of determination and perseverance, and some luck, can become a publishable writer, and what we could do was teach technique. We believed we could help emerging writers become better writers sooner.

Anyone who is literate can write, after all, and if all one wants to do is keep a diary without planning to share it with anyone else, that person does not need help, and studying technique would be wasted effort. Why bother? Write the diary, and be done with it. But as soon as publication is the goal, then technique becomes necessary.

That was our starting point. Next we talked about the kinds of writers we had met and how they worked. Although possibly there are as many methods of writing as there are writers, there is one dichotomy that cannot be denied. There are natural storytellers and there are wordsmiths, and their methods are quite different. Once I walked in on a conversation between two professional writers to hear one say she agonized over which words to use. Even getting someone up from the table and out the door was difficult. The other one said, "Just say he got up and walked out. It's that simple." She looked at him in amazement. For her it certainly was not that simple. There was the difference between a storyteller and a wordsmith.

Damon and I made a pretty good team; he was a wordsmith and I'm a storyteller. I think of it as surface and depth, with the full understanding that it is much more complex than that. But it was a starting point. Damon was a master with the surface, but sometimes if the surface was too bad, he failed to see beyond to the depth. And often I ignored the surface to explore the story I found below.

We realized early that we had to cope with both kinds of writers at Clarion, and what was effective with one was not necessarily effective with the other.

A good story is one in which the surface and depth are fused into one inseparable whole. Beautiful language, unique imagery, subtle symbolism over nothing is not a good story. Neither is a story obscured by bad word choices, awkward phrases that conceal meaning rather than reveal it, inappropriate symbolism or metaphors. We often encountered both types.

Having a group of twenty-five or more people critique a story, pointing out what was good and what was bad was extremely helpful, of course. But the students needed methods they could apply to achieve fusion after they left the group. Too often at home, mother, spouse, beloved-other thought whatever came out of the typewriter—I'm talking BC here, before computers—was wonderful, while the beginning writer was contemplating papering a room with rejection slips.

Those who were blind to the prose had to retrain their brains to look at and consider words instead of yielding to the impulse to write as swiftly as possible and think of the story as done when they reached the end. Continue to write at whatever speed is comfortable, we said, but then apply reason. For those who were blind to the fact that no story lay behind gorgeous language the message was harder: use the language you love, but then search for the meaning. We devised methods for each group without ever mentioning the dichotomy we had seen and were working with. We wanted everyone to try everything.

There is an adage: the more bitter the medicine, the quicker the cure. The exercises that follow are laborious and time consuming; everyone hated doing them, but presumably, after enough doses, they helped cure the problem, or at the very least alleviated it.

Using a finished story, take clean paper and cover everything but one sentence. Read that sentence. Does it say exactly what you intended and nothing else? That's the test. For example: "'Don't do that!' he exploded." Looks okay? Wrong. You can't explode words. You can utter them, say them, mutter, murmur, yell, shout, whisper, and so on. You can't laugh words or giggle words, or ejaculate words, or jump up and down words. Use *say*. If something stronger is needed, go to *yell* or *shout*.

"He looked at the book sitting on the table." Pretty

innocuous? Wrong. Inanimate objects don't sit. Damon used to draw funny little pictures of things sitting around, books with legs dangling over the edge of the table, coffee cups with legs, plates, papers, guns....

Consider this sentence: "Her snakelike walk, gliding sinuously among the tables, was alluring." Look up *sinuous*. Snakelike? Why repeat it? Rephrase.

Or, "The ringing of the bells, clanging in his head, was giving him a headache, and sent him packing." Too many *ing* sounds. Rephrase.

Consider: "Running down the stairs, he put on his shoes and opened the door." I doubt it. You can't do all those things simultaneously.

Forget the story line, the plot, everything about the story except the sentences, and examine them one at a time, and then one word at a time.

Another exercise we tried was meant to curb a tendency toward purple prose; that is, prose in which the modifiers—adjectives and adverbs usually—overwhelm the nouns and verbs. Take them out. All of them. Each and every one of them. Not just the immediate modifiers, but also the modifiers of the modifiers. For example: "The full, ballooning moon, glowing as if alive with white-hot fires forged in an unworldly icy hell, rose serenely with its majestically imperial presence over the harsh, frozen, and hostile tundra." Three or four sentences like that in a row can make the reader lose the story line altogether. Sensory overload sets in with too many images, too many contrasting and competing ideas. Where is the focus of that sentence? What does it actually say and mean? *The moon rose.* Okay, but you might need a little more than that.

After you strip the entire story down to its bare bones, start at the beginning and see just how many of the modifiers you must restore. *The full moon rose over the frozen tundra.* If that is what you need to convey, stop there. Sensory overload can be more deadly to a story than minimalist prose. You may be surprised to find a much stronger story than you started with once it's relieved of its overwhelming finery.

If most of your verbs are paired with adverbs, use stronger verbs. They should not need crutches.

Here is another exercise. The story has a surface that is as flawless as you can make it, and yet the story is unpublishable. One way to find out why is to examine it with a different set of tools. Start with the first paragraph, read it several times, just that one paragraph, and then write in the margin what happens in it or what it is about. You may decide it's a description of the place, the setting. Write *setting.* Next paragraph, do the same thing. More setting? The next and next. You may find that by the end of the story, you have written setting over and over. Or perhaps it was character description, or something else repeated time after time with different phrases but the same basic meaning. The story is static, giving the reader more and more of the same thing glossed with beautiful language. Or maybe there is a character moving through the setting. Same diagnosis: a static story, nothing happens.

A walk through a park, no matter how lovely or dreary the park, is not a story. A character study is not a story. Impeccable language, beautiful imagery will not make them turn into stories. Something has to happen; something has to change. Equilibrium must be upset, either within the story, or in the reader experiencing the story. The end of a story signifies that a new equilibrium has been achieved.

Think of a Pooh stick tossed into a stream where you can watch its progress without knowing if it will land or if it will be destroyed, tumbling this way and that, caught in eddies and swept faster, then slower, but moving until it finishes its journey, always in sight. It has arrived at a new destination, achieved a new equilibrium. There is movement, something happens, and there is an end. The motion is visible, the action is within the story.

There is another kind of story, however, where the stick is tossed into a body of water and there is no apparent motion except for a gentle bobbing. But the currents are strong beneath the surface of the water, and when you turn your gaze away, you realize that the movement, the change has been within you, not in the stick. Something happens; at the end of the story you arrive at a new destination, a new understanding or a new insight, a revelation about an event, a world, or a person. The story of revelation can be extremely powerful, and the appearance of stasis is deceptive. The stick is unmoved; the reader is moved instead. Something happens.

Either of the two examples above could be made into stories if the writer knows in advance what is to be revealed by the end. The walk in the park could be a story if it is revealed that without an exit, an escape route, Eden can be a prison. The character sketch could turn into a story if it is revealed that someone altogether different from the public face lives behind the mask the character wears. But you have to know what the story is about and not simply hope that enough lovely prose will cause something to develop. That takes the guiding hand and head of a writer.

Damon and I lived in a huge, unmanageable, 1890-era Victorian house, with a huge, equally unmanageable-at-times family. On cold nights with snow piling up deeper and deeper, the thermometer plunging to zero or lower, we sat near a fire in a fireplace big enough to roast a pig on a spit, something we discussed doing now and then but never got around to. We talked about everything, including the twists and turns our lives had taken to put us in the role of teachers. How strenuously we both had worked to avoid what we considered to be the teacher trap.

Immediately after graduating from high school, Damon left Hood River, Oregon, the small town where he grew up. His father was principal of the high school, and his mother had been a teacher; he fled and joined the Futurians, a group devoted to science fiction, in New York. The group broke up, each member going his own way after a time, but Damon remained a Futurian in spirit for the rest of his life. He had sidestepped the teacher trap. He knew from an early age that he had to become a writer.

All through my childhood I told stories, and then wrote stories in high school. Several different teachers said I would be a writer and I didn't understand why they did. I knew that writers were magical, godlike, and dead. At least the ones we studied were dead. I did not qualify on any count. Wanting to write stories and becoming a real writer were so far apart, I didn't see how anyone could bridge the gap. I was good in chemistry and math, and I decided to be a chemist until the adviser told me that I would end up as a man's lab assistant or else I would teach. By then I had a college scholarship, but I didn't take advantage of it; instead, I got a job, married, started a family, and tried to read every book in the Louisville Public Library. Ten years after graduating from high school, I was reading an anthology and finished a story I thought was quite bad. I closed the book and said, "I can do that." I wrote a story, rented a typewriter to copy it, mailed it, then wrote another one. I sold them both and bought the typewriter with my first check. I've been writing ever since. I too had avoided the teacher trap.

Yet, there we were, Damon and I, sitting by the fire,

planning our next two weeks as teachers at Clarion, both of us eager to do it again, determined to try harder and do better next time. We had entered the teacher trap unaware; the trap had sprung, and we were captured.

Years Two and Three

W e were back in the charming old resident dorm, still condemned, still empty except for our group. That year Jonathan had a tricycle, and he loved racing through the corridors, around and around in the lounge, and even in the women's wing, where he announced his presence, calling out, "Man on the floor!"

I felt as if time had pulled off another magic trick: the intervening months had been snipped out. This was a continuation of the previous year. We were marginally better prepared, but not yet real teachers. We were still doing very little lecturing, leaving that up to Robin, who was so good at it. But I took a long story I had revised, and we talked about revisions—everything from simple wrong words to paragraphs added, to total rewrites starting with page one, word one. My edited manuscripts were a mess, with additions scrawled in the margins, continued on the reverse side, words and phrases struck out, others inserted illegibly. They still look much like that, in fact.

That year there was another ongoing summer workshop, a class in anthropology, the Diggers, being taught by a man whose degree was in social studies. He wore jodhpurs, high black boots with a mirror shine, and a pith helmet in the wilds of Pennsylvania.

The Diggers were even grimmer than our own students had been the previous year, and several of them began to hang out with our group. They came armed, ready to do battle, and they were accepted. Two of them left anthropology after that summer, went to California, and tried their hands at script writing.

Their instructor came searching for them one afternoon and spotted Russell Bates. "What tribe are you from?" he asked. Russell said Kiowa. The instructor grasped his chin, turned his head this way and that, and said, "You could be." He invited Russell to come see his collection of Indian skulls. With admirable restraint Russell politely declined.

Russell had traveled to Clarion with a trunkload of fireworks. On the Fourth of July, the president of the college had an evening social, and while people were sitting around having a civilized conversation over their gin and tonic, there came a series of explosions. The party froze; the president turned livid, and our man on the spot, Robin, did not say a word, although he muttered under his breath, "I'm going to kill that Indian."

Russell had led a group to the nearby cemetery, where they celebrated Independence Day.

We muddled our way through as before, a little better at explaining our critiques and generalizing from them. We invited the students to sign up for private conferences, but we did not demand that everyone do so. We had started to read all the previous stories, and we were prepared to talk about them as a whole, not just the stories we had workshopped. And we gave them the assignments we had worked out for examining their own stories, line by line, paragraph by paragraph, after they left Clarion. Without quite realizing it, we were laying the groundwork for what was to become our normal procedures in the following years.

We felt we had done a little bit better than before, but

not enough better, and still did not know exactly what to do differently.

In the sixties I developed an allergy that affected my eyes and resulted in three surgeries. My ophthalmologist sent me to an ocular allergist in New York City—I had never heard of such a specialty before. That doctor failed to diagnose the cause of my problem, but he prescribed a desensitizing program—injections to be administered by my own doctor in Milford—and we all hoped that would take care of it. However, I reacted severely to the third shot, and my doctor refused to continue the program. At that time the only advice anyone could offer was for me to leave the area on the chance that the allergy was environment-caused.

We had completed that year's Milford Conference and Clarion, and we decided to go to Florida for the coming winter. James Sallis, his former wife, and their child, along with Tom Disch, rented our house for the period. Both Jim and Tom had been frequent visitors, and it seemed ideal all around.

In Florida we rented a dilapidated two-story beach house in which we sat out a hurricane that fall. All day the weather advisories had said the hurricane would make landfall up in the panhandle, that the beaches would be subjected to high tides, but nothing more. Late in the day, with the streets flooded and water rising, a fire truck rolled by with a bullhorn advising immediate evacuation. The storm would come ashore a few miles north of Clearwater, thirty miles north of us. At the same time the television advisories were telling everyone not to drive on flooded streets, and not to attempt to cross any of the bridges to the mainland. Not exactly rock and hard place, but rather hurricane winds and flooding. Unable to drive out, we sat in the upstairs of our old house and alternated between watching rising water out the windows and *Star Trek* on television, interrupted continuously by new advisories.

The water rose to the doorsill, stopped, and gradually subsided. We knew how lucky we had been.

That fall and winter, my eye problem vanished, and we had a very hard decision to make: try Milford again and hope there was no recurrence, or remain in Florida. We opted to go home.

We returned in time to do Milford, and later to go back to Clarion for the third time. We found changes that year. We were still in the condemned building, but the students were housed in different quarters: a bleak and loveless concrete block building that had all the characteristics of a prison. The rooms were tiny and airless, there was no real gathering place, no wide porch and surrounding shrubbery for water gun battles; but there was a dorm manager who clearly did not approve of the workshop attendees and their unconventional behavior. Probably he did not approve of long hair on males, but that was never actually stated. He, of course, was called the Warden. Our group then—and for many years afterward—was eyed with suspicion. Robin told me that various people asked him who was that woman in blue jeans with the baby and what was she doing on campus. Damon with his long hair, I in blue jeans, rowdy students armed with water guns and superballs, none of us was quite proper, clearly out of place in an academic setting.

Nothing about the town had changed, and it still had little to offer in the way of entertainment and diversion. In spite of all that, the workshop was as successful as it had been previously, the students as talented, hardworking, and as determined as ever.

By the third year, it was undeniable that the workshop was doing something right. Former students were writing stories, selling them, getting published. Many of them were becoming professional writers. What combination of talent, teachers, environment, and dedication proved the potent magic mix was impossible to tell, but it was effective then and on through the years. We suspected that the array of teachers, each one bringing a different perspective, demanding quality work, concentrating on whatever aspect of writing that particular writer-teacher saw as of primary importance, had a great influence on the success of the workshop as a whole.

During the long talks we had had over our roles, Damon and I came to realize that many of the students had no clear understanding of what was meant by a short story. We decided that would be our starting point that summer. After all, the workshop was for short story writers.

A short story is a narrative work of fiction under an arbitrary length that is variable depending on who is counting and for what purposes. For the genre-writing awards it is accepted that the cut-off for short stories is 7,500 words. A novelette is from 7,500 words to about 15,000. A novella is from 15,000 to 40,000 words, and a novel is 40,000 words and up. Although they all share the term narrative fiction, they differ substantially.

A novel opens a door into another world and invites the reader to enter and explore it with the writer. Whether the other world is on a different planet, in a different period of time, or is placed here and now, it is always a different world. Each writer interprets the experienced world differently; no two are exactly alike. Actually the only new thing writers have to offer is their own perception of a world as it exists or is imagined.

In the novel, plots and subplots and usually many characters are developed and often many viewpoints are used. There is no time or space restriction; the writer is free to wander through the past, the present, the future, and roam the entire universe if the novel requires it. A novel is a forgiving form of fiction and for many reasons, excluding length, the easiest to write.

A novella usually has one main story line that is developed thoroughly, with minor subplots that are often hinted at rather than explicated. The novel opens a world; the novella opens a piece of it. Hemingway's *The Old Man and the Sea* is a good example. Much of Henry James's work is in the novella form. There can be several characters who weave in and out of the main story line with their own viewpoints taken, and even minor subplots explored.

A novelette is more restricted, usually has one main character, and a story line that is followed from start to finish with few diversions. The form allows for room to explore yet a smaller piece of the world, only that part that is important to the story, although that abbreviated part may be well developed.

A successful short story is a marvel of compression, nuance, inference and suggestion. If the novel invites one to enter another world, the short story invites one to peer through a peephole into the world, and yet the world has to have the same reality as in a novel. It truly is the universe in a grain of sand. This is done by compression and implication. Every single word has to help the story, or it hurts it. The short story is the least forgiving form of narrative fiction, with no room for redundancies, for backing up to explain what was meant before, for auctorial intrusions that may be perfectly allowable in the novel.

That is one reason why the flashback, useful in novels, is most often a mistake for the short story. There is not enough space allowed to go over the same territory twice. Again and again students applied novelistic techniques to the short story, and failed invariably.

In the short story, there must be the moment of truth. There must be something important at stake for the characters within the world of the story to which they react in meaningful ways; or there has to be a moment of truth in which the reader comes to realize what is at stake even if the story characters remain oblivious. Someone has to react to the moment of truth of the story.

If there is no moment of truth, if the choice before the hero is between vanilla and chocolate, the story is trivial. An anecdote, no matter how cute or charming, is trivial in this context. A character study is most often trivial. That came to be one of the most dreaded words of the workshop, that single word *trivial* written on the manuscript. Damon's *So what?* was possibly even more devastating.

Up until and even including the third year, Damon and I reacted to the stories, explained our reasoning as best we could, and moved on. Sometime during that third year, too late to do much about it, we came to the realization that our approach had been wrong from the start. As I mentioned earlier, we had been treating these beginning writers the way the professional writers at the Milford Conference treated each other, and we found that not only was it not appropriate, but it likely was confusing, as well. With professional writers who had learned and assimilated methods and techniques through the years, it was rarely necessary to explain anything. It was enough to say the story dragged in the middle, or the ending was too rushed, or something of that sort, and depend on the writer to solve the problem, if that writer agreed it was a problem. They never mistook anecdotes or vignettes for stories, or wrote trivial stories, or mixed up viewpoints, or made the many mistakes beginning writers make. Trial and error is unforgiving as a teacher. With beginning writers, an explanation is necessary if they are going to avoid the years of rejections that would also serve as teachers. We realized we were dealing with the same problems repeatedly and we had failed to anticipate and prepare for them, but in year three, with four weeks of teaching experience behind us, we were still workshopping individual stories and hoping the students would generalize for themselves. That was not enough. They needed to be told in detail why certain beginnings would not work, or why the middle dragged, or the ending failed. They needed some explicit rules that would apply to most stories, not only to the one specific story in hand. Those lessons had to be thought through, then articulated in a comprehensible way, not done as an overnight chore.

During the first year or two, some of the students never said a word in our presence outside of the workshop proper. Too shy? Intimidated? We didn't know exactly why, but we wanted to get to know each one of them as individuals. We invited them to sign up to talk to us if they wanted to discuss problems. Most of them took advantage of our offer, and we began what were to become routine individual conferences. Because there were still some who did not sign up for appointments, we dropped the invitation and began passing out a sign-up sheet, and said everyone had to come by. That filled our afternoons to overflowing, but it was a good thing to do. Often we could see a pattern after reading several stories by a student, something that would not have been revealed in a single story. It also made it necessary for us to curtail the nearly all-night talk and play sessions we had been enjoying with them. Keeping up with the reading, preparing for the coming day, breathing; all took time. And then there was sleep to try to get in.

That year we came across several stories with impossible actions, and we paired off the writers and had them try to demonstrate the positions protagonists within the stories were said to have taken. Often the impossible actions were things happening simultaneously. There was a near catastrophe when one student, enacting his story, tried to run out the door, kiss his girlfriend, and put on his shoes all at the same time. One young man tried valiantly to grab his partner by the uvula and kiss her. We also had them read dialogue and in both demonstrations, good points were made. Use a dictionary, for starters, and visualize the scene. Listen to the dialogue in your head, or read it aloud in the privacy of your room with the window and door closed. It was great fun for everyone, except the hapless student who came near to getting his face slapped when he started to reach for the wrong body part.

I realized that year that not everyone played scenes in their heads the way I always had done. It came as a surprise to me. Afterward I urged them to take each part in every major scene and play it mentally over and over, seeing how it would look from the eyes of A, then B, C, and so on. Assuming the viewpoint of one who is not the protagonist, and possibly is the antagonist, is good practice.

For those students who didn't visualize scenes, I suggested that a harder, more laborious view, would be to write a few scenes from the different characters' viewpoints. I doubted that many of them attempted it after a time or two. That is real work.

Another thing we came to realize was that the good basic five W's of journalism apply equally to writing fiction. Who? Where? What? When? Why? They don't have to be in that order, but they have to be given, or implied—and the sooner, the better. Especially the *who* question. Out there in the world, seventh-grade teachers stress the need to start with a dramatic scene to capture the attention of a reader, and consequently there are a lot of stories that start with bullets whizzing over someone's head, or someone running for his life, or a different dramatic situation equally empty. *Who is this?* was often our notation in the margin of those stories. And why should I care if someone I don't know is fleeing from an unknown menace?

If a story starts with the most powerful image, or the most dramatic scene, it has only one direction it can take: downward. A story of diminishing interest is a failure. Instead, it should develop naturally to that moment of greatest interest. Also, if it starts with the most dramatic incident, there is all that backtracking that must be done to explain how it came about that the bullets began to whiz, and then what can you do? Repeat the opening scene? Trust the reader to remember the details? Skip it?

It's best to avoid that dilemma altogether. Start with a character and a place. Trust the reader to carry on for a time at least. For the doubtful, I suggest a good anthology of short stories as a source to confirm that this simple technique works beautifully. Story after story will start with a character in a particular place, and we, the readers, are grounded in the reality of the fictional world with a person. Who and where are all important, too important to work in later. The other W's will be answered in their own good time.

I'll come back to the five W's often, with explicit lessons we developed, but that third year at Clarion, we did not have those lessons yet. Students were learning how to become writers; we were learning how to become teachers.

When the final week was winding down, Gardner Dozois came to visit. Damon had bought a story from Gardner for his *Orbit* series of anthologies while Gardner was still in Germany after mustering out of the army. We invited him to visit as in Milford, when he returned to the States, and one day he showed up, a tall, gaunt, cadaverous, specter-at-the-wedding figure, dressed in a long black raincoat, black boots, with a wild ginger-red beard, and a wicked sense of humor. He stayed with us for weeks before leaving for New York to begin a career that led to him becoming one of the field's most respected editors.

No one had invited him to visit Clarion, but there he was. He was a tremendous hit with the students. On Saturday, everyone was to gather in the lounge to go to Robin's house for the going-away party. Damon and I were in the lounge waiting for the gang when we heard a god-awful noise coming down the street. Gardner was leading the students in a parade, all chanting the monkey chant from *The Wizard of Oz*, and six of the men were carrying a "virgin" on their shoulders. (They later declared that the hardest part of the parade was finding a virgin.) They came to a stop outside the lounge, and Gardner proceeded to dig out the virgin's heart with a butter knife and then hold it aloft with a triumphant howl.

Minutes later, Robin dashed into the lounge. "Katie," he said, "is it true? She had a candle in her thingie?"

"Yes, Robin. But it wasn't lit."

"Thank God!"

The parade had passed under the president's window, and he was not amused.

I have never suggested or even hinted that Gardner was the reason why that was our last year at Clarion State College. But I confess I have always wondered.

That was Robin's last year at the college. He was moving up in the world of academia, a series of moves that eventually saw him installed as president of Chico State College in California. That was also the last Clarion Workshop in Pennsylvania. We were dismayed; the wonderful experiment had come to an end. The most successful writing workshop ever imagined, demonstrably successful in the work the students continued to do, the publishing records they were establishing, was over. At the time, it seemed hopeless to consider an alternative academic sponsor capable of organizing it at a different institution; we had to accept its demise, and although bereft and grieving, we also felt a tremendous gratitude that we had been a small part of it.

Two New Homes

Within weeks of returning home from that last Clarion, my allergy reasserted itself. We knew we had to make a permanent move. It was not an easy choice. Milford is seventy miles from New York City, an easy drive, and there is reliable bus and train service. We had a lot of company there, weekend guests, sometimes weeks-long guests. It was a wonderful place to hold the Milford Conference. We both loved our impossible house: a haunted basement, and three and a half floors, all filled. When we put it up for sale, we had a house-cleaning orgy. Damon cleared one closet three times, and then I cleared it again. It was like that throughout. We sold the house in January and moved to Madeira Beach, Florida.

Meanwhile on the West Coast, Vonda McIntyre was working hard to establish and find support for a second Clarion Workshop: Clarion West. I asked her how it happened that she undertook such a mammoth task. Here is her answer:

Clarion State College, Clarion Pennsylvania, 1970.

I dragged into town after an unexpected night in Pittsburgh during which I read everything I had with me to read. That was the last moment to drag, because the Clarion Writers Workshop began the next day. The six weeks were an amazing experience. Other sections in this book will describe it, so I'll skip to the end when we found out that the director, Robin Scott Wilson, was moving to Chicago for the next academic year, and Clarion Writers Workshop in Pennsylvania would be no more.

I couldn't bear that idea, and neither could Jim Sallis, who visited the 1970 workshop and sat in on some of the sessions. Robin gave Jim and me his blessing to try to set up branches of the Clarion Workshop at other universities, and we all (reluctantly) went home.

It's been so long since the first incarnation of Clarion West—1971–1973—that it's hard to remember the names of the people at the University of Washington who helped get it going. I haven't forgotten their patience with my inexperience, and their support. Somehow it all came together. It was a different mix than Clarion, Pennsylvania. Almost all the writers in residence were from the West Coast. The program included some authors who had never taught workshops before and who turned out to be wonderful, such as Ursula K. Le Guin. The class was smaller than average because of the haste with which everything got put together and advertised. It was a little bit shaky, I'm afraid, but the students griped some, laughed, shrugged off a certain amount of unavoidable adversity, and wrote. And wrote. And wrote.

I pulled out my first gray hair (I was twenty two) and pasted it to the wall where I could point it out to people. (I never confessed that premature gray hair is a common characteristic of my mother's family.)

Ursula gave me a poster to put on my door. Two vultures surveyed a barren desert. Vulture One to Vulture Two: "Patience, my ass. I'm going to kill someone."

Lin Nielsen, one of the students, was a major factor in the workshop's success, and I'll always be grateful to her for pitching in. I was trying to be a graduate student that first summer (not having quite yet realized that as a research scientist, I made a very good sf writer), and I believe I was just a trifle nutsoid.

The West Coast workshop instituted an innovation that I think has served it well: the sponsoring departments asked the workshop to offer something open to the public, and so the Tuesday-night reading series began. It continues to this day, courtesy of the Elliott Bay Book Company and, in recent years, the University Book Store and its sf/f manager, Duane Wilkins.

The workshop continued in 1972 and 1973, at the University of Washington. I think it was a terrific trio of workshops. I fondly remember sitting in the courtyard of Hansee Hall doing writing exercises set by Ursula K. Le Guin. Avram Davidson put together a particularly effective experiment, which started out with all of us wandering off to lunch bitching and moaning about the impossibility of doing what he'd asked us to do (write stories inspired by random words drawn from, first, a pile of technical words, and, second, a pile of domestic words), and ended up with half a dozen published stories, including "Of Mist,

Grass, and Sand," which a couple of years later evolved into *Dreamsnake*.

After three summers, I understood why Robin had moved to Chicago. I felt burned out, and couldn't afford the time or energy (or the relatively low pay of a conference organizer) to keep doing it. I moved to Oregon and lived in a cabin four miles down a logging road for a couple of years, courtesy of some dear friends who swear to this day that the pittance I was paying them for rent reallio trulio did pay the mortgage.

Some years later, J. T. Stewart, Clarion '71 (now a professor at Fairhaven College, Western Washington University), and Marilyn Holt (now the president of the northwest chapter of Mystery Writers of America) said to me, "We have this great idea. We'd like to revive Clarion West." I said, "I know a good shrink I could refer you to." But they did revive it, in 1984, and it's continued strong ever since, as a nonprofit organization run by a dynamic group of volunteers.

But that's *their* story.

While that was going on, to our astonishment and delight, we learned that James Sallis had come to the rescue for *our* Clarion. He had become a graduate student at Tulane University in New Orleans, and that was where the next Clarion Workshop was held in 1971. We were invited to participate. And against all odds, we were again within driving distance.

The session in New Orleans remains a blur in many ways. By the time we arrived, Jim Sallis had become ill, and we didn't even see him; the academic director was not around, and we were left on our own with the students. If Clarion, Pennsylvania, had been a wasteland with nothing to do, New Orleans proved to be the polar opposite, with far too much to lure students away. It is said of New Orleans that one can't throw a stick without hitting a restaurant with excellent food reasonably priced. Damon became ill from eating soft-shelled crabs, and said he would do it again. They were so good, it was a small price to pay. Jonathan broke out in giant hives, from food, water, something, possibly the roaches that were three to four inches long and were called palmetto bugs. But they were roaches on steroids. We could hear them galloping around at night. Harlan Ellison left us a can of insect spray with instructions not to spray the creatures, but to beat them to death with the can. Some of the students visited a local cemetery, where they were intrigued to learn that no one is buried underground, the water table is so high that coffins tend to float. Instead, the interments are above ground, and the area is swarming with lizards. They caught a lot of lizards and brought them back to the university and put them to work catching and eating the roaches—excuse me, palmetto bugs. Lizards ran and scampered everywhere all the time we were there.

The French Quarter, with easy access by streetcar, was irresistible to many of the students. We met some of our students on arrival and never saw them again until the going-away party.

For many years it was accepted that the class had to have twenty-five students to cover the costs. That was an inhuman workload for everyone, students and teachers alike. Some of the twenty-five warm bodies that year had registered only because they earned college credits for a class they could skip without penalty. But the hard core, those who had come to learn something about writing, were as hardworking and dedicated as ever, and we worked as hard as ever, too.

We had been warned that Louisiana was particularly keen on enforcing drug laws and that the penalties were harsh, with jail time the norm. That was 1971, in the middle of the hip years, the turn-off, tune-in, drop-out years. Some of our students certainly heard that message and measured up wholeheartedly if not admirably. They smoked pot in the dorm. One of the younger Clarion students, a strong law'n order type, reported them to campus security and in panic someone called us. Damon and I rushed up to the dorm floor, lit cigarettes, and tried to fill the corridor with smoke. I lit a small fire in a waste can and doused it with water, adding more smoke. When the security man arrived, I said I had accidentally started a fire and I pointed to the can. He looked at me, I looked at him, and we both knew I was lying. He glanced over the students gathered in the hall, looking guilty as sin, told us to watch it, and left. Crisis over.

Then we gave them hell for endangering the whole program. If there had been a drug bust, I had no doubt that Clarion would have been finished for all time.

During this period, Robin Scott Wilson had met R. Glenn Wright and Leonard Isaacs, who both taught at Justin Morrill College, a small college within the Michigan State University. Glenn was an English professor and Lenny a molecular biologist who wrote very good poetry, and both had an interest in science fiction and fantasy. Justin Morrill College was dedicated to the idea of introducing humanities students to the rigors of math and science, and science majors to the arts and letters. There were many such experimental colleges springing up in the early seventies, daring in many ways, and mostly successful in bridging the gap between the sciences and the humanities that C. P. Snow had written about.

Glenn Wright and Lenny Isaacs were interested in becoming directors of the workshop, with Justin Morrill College as its host, sponsored by the university, and from 1972 until many years later, that was the workshop's home.

Glenn had a mop of curly-frizzy hair, an unholy twinkle in his eyes, and a decidedly perverse sense of humor. He was very strongly built, slender but muscular, with wide shoulders. He loved his students, and they returned that love. He was also a very good cook, and we delighted in the many meals he prepared for us over the years. Lenny, less the extrovert, was a brilliant intellectual who loved puns. He also had a wonderful sense of humor, a dry humor that caught one unaware more often than not. He never cooked a meal, and in fact had carpeted over his stove and kept books in the oven, where they were safe from the elements. He was a true gourmet and a wine connoisseur. Both of them were extremely good critics, and both were very good at working university politics. Glenn enjoyed doing battle with the powers in charge, and he enjoyed more the many victories he won along the way. Lenny did not like the political scene, and as a result often was more efficient in getting things done than Glenn was, simply because he wanted to put it behind him as quickly as possible. They both became powerful early advocates within MSU for Clarion, and without them, it is doubtful Clarion would have survived.

I came to realize what a sacrifice it was for a full-time professor to give up half of the summer to participate in Clarion. Glenn and Lenny were both single, in no great need of the additional pay, and the Clarion duties they alternated taking were not simply six weeks of work. For a number of years, the director was the sole judge of the applicants' stories. There were dorm managers to approach, parking arrangements to be made, much paperwork to register twenty to twenty-five summer students, the visiting lecturers to approach and engage, travel arrangements, schedules, and so forth. Then there were the emergencies that arose after the workshop began. One year it was a broken arm of a student who had been demonstrating how to ascend a chimney in mountain climbing. Once a visiting lecturer became ill at three in the morning. I lost a crown one year and had to see a dentist. A student had to leave for a family emergency; she had to be taken to the airport, then met and brought back a few days later. The director was always on hand to take care of such things, day or night. It was a great deal of work, and the directors were marvelous at seeing that it got done.

Not all the directors sat in on all of the workshop sessions during our two weeks each year, but both Glenn and Lenny did, and their critiques ranged from brilliant to farcical. At one time, critiquing a story, Lenny started with the Babylonian civilization, advanced to Greece, the conquest by the Roman Empire, the Ottoman Empire, and up through the ages to present time, then concluded: "And when I read your story, I felt the entire Western Civilization come crashing down on my head." It was a marvelous speech which got him a round of applause. The student being skewered was laughing hysterically.

I used to read tarot cards for the students in those early years. No one took it seriously; it was fun and games, an ice breaker. I seldom remembered afterward what I had read in the cards. At a party in Glenn's house in 1972, I read the cards for one student after another with the expected cards of uncertainty, indecision, confusion, and so on turning up. Then a dapper man in a business suit complete with tie asked if I would read for him. I remember him particularly as being very clean and neat. The students, Damon, and I, were all scruffy, sweaty, exhausted. The students, who liked to watch the Tarot readings, were clustered around as the neat man sat opposite me and shuffled the cards, and everyone could see that his cards were completely different from those that had been falling earlier. Glenn said later I had told this gentleman that he was in the middle of a business deal that had him concerned, but that it would have a very satisfactory outcome, and that it would be resolved within the next two weeks.

I might have said that—I don't remember. That was my introduction to Dr. Herman King, who was acting provost of summer programming. He became another powerful advocate for Clarion until his retirement. Without his strong commitment to Clarion, it would have folded for lack of funding many times over. Glenn also told me that I had been right in what I said: Herman was in the middle of a deal that turned out well for him within the two weeks I had mentioned.

A few years later I received a letter from a woman who had been at Clarion the previous summer. She said everything I told her had come to pass: Her live-in boyfriend had beaten her up, threatened her life, and kicked her out. Although I did not remember what I had read, I knew I had not said anything like that. I never read the cards at Clarion again. By the time we arrived, the students were too fragile psychologically to risk subjecting them to anything that could possibly be disturbing, or that they could interpret as disturbing. The tarot cards, crystal ball gazing, palmistry—all could be misinterpreted wildly.

Robin Scott Wilson, who continued to teach the first week for years after he stopped being the director, Glenn Wright, Leonard Isaacs, and Herman King were the four pillars that bore the burden of keeping the workshop alive and functioning during those shaky early years through crises, funding alarms, irate dorm managers' complaints, whatever came along to threaten its existence.

The housing at MSU was in high-rise brick buildings, all more or less alike, all with equally bad food in the cafeterias. Segregation was still the norm in those years. Males in one wing, females in another, or on separate floors. One year, the worst, they had the women housed in a different building altogether. There were only five or six women that year, and eighteen or twenty men, and the dorms were locked at ten every night. To gain entrance after ten, one had to ring the bell, wait for someone to identify him or her and open the door. At the same time, there were advisories that women were not to be out after dark except in groups, because there was a rapist on campus. The students were always encouraged to consult one another, to brainstorm ideas, to seek information from anyone who could supply it, and there was always a convivial group for discussions and play. The women, quite rightly, felt excluded from much of the group activities that year.

Michigan State occupies a vast area, with pleasant walks to the horticultural gardens, greenhouses, library, swimming pool, and so on. A brown river meanders through the campus with many bridges, canoeing, ducks to feed, all in all a lovely parklike setting. There are trees imported from around the world, neatly labeled, black squirrels scampering here and there, a bell tower chiming the time, and town close by.

East Lansing has good bookstores, fine restaurants, fast food, enough distraction to occupy idle hours, not enough to keep students out all night sightseeing, or doing whatever they had found to do in New Orleans. It was the ideal workshop setting, except for the housing and segregation and terrible dorm food. But students and faculty alike considered that the norm.

For years it seemed that no dorm manager was willing to have the Clarion group back a second time. Too disruptive, too much complaining about food or something else, up until all hours, water gun fights in the halls, Frisbee games in the underground passages . . . Just too much. So we moved a lot.

In those years, Damon and I walked every inch of the

campus. We talked about the lessons we had given, or those to come. We talked about how to get through to a student who kept repeating the same kind of dead-end story, how to encourage another one, what we had to improvise to meet a challenge we had not anticipated. . . . We talked about everything as we walked. We never knew if we would be back the following year, or if we had to try to cover everything we knew this year, as there might never be another chance.

We never consulted about stories to be workshopped. We had separate opinions, separate assessments about what needed to be done, sometimes quite opposite each other's. That was valuable, too. Art appreciation is always subjective, and story critiques were also subjective once the basics were covered—grammar, technical problems, fixable surface problems.

One thing we agreed upon early and never wavered about was the need for absolute honesty. It was often difficult to be totally honest about a story that was a dismal failure with no redeeming value. We heard about other teachers who made it a point to find and praise something good in every story, but if we didn't find anything to praise, we passed and pointed out why it failed. We both said from the start that the workshop was not a high school or even a standard college creative-writing course where students who knew which end of the pencil wrote were praiseworthy. We decided it was better to hear unpleasant truth from us, people who were ready to offer advice and help, than to infer it from years of rejection slips that offered no clues as to why. As a result, some students regarded us as too harsh, too hard, and possibly we were, but we also explained that they were there because they had talent, they had things to say and were in the process of acquiring the skill with which to say it, and we had very high expectations for them. We expected them to reach beyond their grasp, to meet those expectations.

I told them that one day when they were feeling particularly low and depressed, to go to the library and look around. All those books were written by individuals who started where they were, at the bottom, rejected, unwanted, unloved, too depressed to continue at times, and yet . . . There they were; there were the works they produced, their books loved by many, read, reread, preserved through the years. Sit down and let yourself feel the presence of all those writers who also struggled, and who persevered and whose works live on after them.

Those Cryptic Marks

I was surprised by how many of the Clarion students had not yet mastered the tools of the trade. Damon had been an editor for years and was not a bit surprised; he had seen it all in submitted manuscripts. Because we didn't want to take class time to teach things like grammar and basic technique, we used abbreviations on the manuscripts and prepared handouts to explain them.

Vp. Viewpoint. Once you've decided whose story this is, the next decision is which viewpoint to use. Generally the one with the most to gain or lose is the logical one for whose story it is. And the viewpoint can be first, second, or third person. After the choice is made, either very consciously or intuitively, the rule is to stick to that viewpoint.

It doesn't stop with the simple choice of person, but goes a little deeper with the additional choice of how objective or subjective to make that viewpoint, or if it will be an omniscient viewpoint.

With the first person objective viewpoint you can tell only what the *I* character can see or hear, no thoughts, no feelings, memories, nothing at all interior. Think of it as a camera/tape recorder perched on the shoulder of the viewpoint character and tell only what the camera sees and the tape recorder hears.

The first person subjective can be as interior as you want

it, all the way to a stream of consciousness, plus whatever is out there in the world, but again it is limited to that one person, the *I* of the story.

In third person objective, you are restricted to what the character, he or she, sees or hears; nothing interior is allowed. In either first or third person, the true objective viewpoint is extremely rare, and most viewpoints that are called objective are not really. They tend to be fairly objective, but with a few interior observations or thoughts used when needed.

The subjective third person has the freedom of going inward. This is a viewpoint limited to one person, as above, but it is much easier to master, since you can see more and explain more about the character, by revealing her thoughts. Often, in order to get in a description of some sort, the novice writer, and too often the more advanced writer, feels a compulsion to have a character brush back his black hair, or rub his blue eyes, or else look in a mirror and tell the reader what is seen there. If there is a need to describe the character it is much better technique to simply come out and do it in the auctorial voice. For example: "John was a solidly built young man of twenty-five, with unruly black hair and bright blue eyes that protruded slightly. He was walking briskly that day when..." Then get on with the story from his viewpoint.

In short fiction, this viewpoint is almost always a single one, but it can be a serial viewpoint, first one person then another, as long as that is quickly established.

The problems that arose usually had to do with shifting viewpoints. A simple scenario can demonstrate what I mean. There is a bank teller, a robber, and a guard, and a robbery is about to take place. Say you've chosen Mary as the viewpoint character, third person, subjective, and there has been introductory material before this sentence. "She was watching the minute hand inch forward, with three minutes to go until quitting time, when he entered. The hand holding his gun was sweating as he glanced about nervously."

One of us, or more likely both of us, would have put *vp* over the phrase, *hand holding his gun was sweating*. It has suddenly become a mixed viewpoint. She can't tell that his hand is sweating, although she could intuit that his glance about is nervous. We have been clued that it is her story, and that it is third person subjective, since we know that she is thinking that it is close to quitting time. It is jarring then to have a second viewpoint enter. Momentarily the writer lost control of the material.

If your intention was to establish an omniscient viewpoint and we will get to know all three characters instead of just one, that intent has to be made in the beginning, not paragraphs into the story.

Frequently the problem would be something like the following: "She was thinking that she would hold her temper this time when she got home. I won't yell about anything. I won't complain...." Suddenly the third person has become a first person for no apparent reason. This could be rephrased simply: "She would not yell about anything, or complain...."

Or, Mary is wrapping up her work and glances at Hal the guard. "He shifted his feet and checked his watch against the clock on the wall. His bunion hurt and he wanted to go home as much as she did. Two minutes later, she looked up and saw John enter and glance about nervously." We have the guard's viewpoint in that section.

Sometimes the criticisms, as in the above, appeared to be petty, not important enough to draw attention to, but we insisted that it was a matter of control. The writer has to learn to control the material and not allow mistakes or carelessness to creep in. Enough of these little things in a story can cause a reader to become uneasy without ever knowing why, and often that uneasiness will lead to deciding the story really was not good enough to continue reading.

WT. Wrong tense. Another common problem we hoped to solve with handouts. In most stories, past tense indicates the present of the story. It is a convention of fiction that we accept it as the ongoing action.

"He ran home." Since we don't know what will follow, this becomes the "now" of the story.

"He was running home," is a continuing action, usually followed by something that happens while he is running. "He was running home when he fell."

"He had run home before." An action in the past of the story takes a past perfect verb.

That past perfect verb seems to throw a curve at many novice writers. And it can cause considerable confusion about when things happen. If he ran home, as above on page one, and a page or two later we read, "He ran home," the question arises, when? You already told us that on page one, or if this is a different time, when was it?

The present tense story is equally simple.

"He runs home."

"He is running home."

"He ran home yesterday." In this case you go to simple past tense.

"He has run home many times."

WN. Wrong number. The wrong verb for the subject. A singular subject takes a singular verb; a plural subject takes a plural verb form. "A simple declarative sentence is never a problem, but with clauses and modifying phrases, they can become problems." That sentence is wrong, of course. The subject of the sentence is *sentence;* the verb must be singular. A simple rephrasing might be "A simple declarative sentence often becomes a problem when clauses and modifying phrases are added."

We saw that often.

A circled word meant "spell it out." Often it was a number written as a numeral when it should have been spelled out, as in dialogue especially, and even more often it was a contraction. "He wouldn't've gone." You have to stop and puzzle it out to learn that it should be, "He would not have gone." Or, "I gotta go now." You might hear that, but don't write it. It offends the eye, and not everyone says it or hears it that way. Gotta, wanna, gonna, all colloquial language of this sort should be spelled out correctly. Some purists maintain that in the narrative, nothing should be contracted with an apostrophe, and its use in dialogue should be limited.

WW. The wrong word was used. Often it is one of a pair of sound-alike words: hear/here, there/their, one/won, its/it's, and so on. The spell checker won't spot them since they are equally good words. Or it could be the more troublesome words: like/such as, then/than, lie/lay, sit/set. There are a lot of them to watch out for. We came to recognize that the lie/lay problem was endemic, but we fought it in our first year, and we were still fighting it in our last.

SP. Spelling. Some of the above words, others that were simply spelled incorrectly or typos.

( ). Parentheses always meant "cut this." It might have been a single word, a phrase, paragraph, or even pages. Redundancies, as in similar thoughts repeated with new phrasing, exact repetitions of language, taking sentences a beat too far, explaining at length

what was self-explanatory, plot loops, various diversions, empty words, and so on. *Horrible* is a good example of an empty word. "He looked at the scene; it was horrible." That tells me nothing. *Horrible* can mean different things to different people. Horrible how? The message was to make the story as tight as possible and still say what needed saying. One woman wrote Damon a note of complaint; he had cut half her story. He corrected her note and returned it, replete with parentheses.

There were what I came to think of as land bridges. An underlined word or phrase, a line drawn to the next example of the same thing, then again, and often many times again. The repetition of a particular sentence structure becomes annoying fast. "He wanted to go but it was too late." "He had enough money but he had to make it last." "He could have gone in but he had not done so."

More commonly it was a simple declarative sentence structure used over and over: Subject, verb, object. Dick and Jane prose. The writer falls into a pattern without noticing. Those lines zigzagging down the page get her attention. Sometimes it is a single word repeated many times when rephrasing would eliminate the problem. If there is only one word that will do, then by all means use it. Usually that is not the case. The dreadful *-ly* words, every verb leaning on an adverb, or *-ing* words, or too many sibilants strung together, or any sound repeated too often.

Often something would be underlined with the note *Not simultaneously* in the margin, or more likely, *Not simul.* Example: "Running down the stairs he dashed to his car and fled." Not at the same time as running down the stairs.

Jingle/jangle, or *JJ* in the margin with words underlined. Sometimes two or more words rhymed. "Fred said" is a classic example, but they often got a bit more complicated. One short paragraph might have included words like Fred, said, head, dead, led, and the like. The eye can skip over them, but if you read it out loud, your ear will catch them. Rephrase.

We didn't put in much class time on any of the above. We assumed that anyone who wants to become a writer would take the time, and make the effort, to learn to use the tools of the trade. Sometimes we recommended a basic English grammar textbook to a student who was starting from way back.

Some students pointed out that published works often had many of the above lapses, sometimes even best-sellers did. I concede the point, and at the same time maintain that it is easier to break a habit before it becomes ingrained than later. Also, each story has to pass the eyes of an editor, one who may be as crotchety as Damon about the prose, or one who may be too overworked to bother with the extent of time-consuming line editing required for an unknown writer yet to prove himself.

I also admit that the surface, the prose, did not bother me as much as it might have if there was a compelling story lurking beneath it. I always assumed that the surface could be fixed, preferably by the writer, but a badly flawed story probably could not be. Damon was far more skeptical that a good story could be badly written.

We were always more interested in the story structure, the characters, setting, and meaning, and those were the areas where we put most of our energy.

All too often one or the other of us, or more likely both, wrote in the margin on the bottom of page two, "What is this about?" You have half a page for page one; the top half is reserved for editorial notes. The first full page of text is number two, and by the end of that full page there should be a clear idea of what the story is about, who is involved, and enough about the setting so that we know where we are. If the same question is posed on page three, four, and so on, the story is in deep trouble. Usually, if a story emerges finally, the problem is structural. It is as if the writer is dancing around the subject matter, uncertain how to start, or else is uncertain what the story is about until many pages into it.

Say it is a twelve-page story, and on page one Leroy emerges from the subway and wanders down the street, then stops in a bar for a drink. There is a little idle chitchat in the bar, he leaves and continues down the street to a store where he buys a loaf of bread, and maybe passes the time of day with the clerk. Back out to wander some more, and page two is over.

We know nothing about Leroy, the neighborhood, what the story is about, or anything else.

If the story is going to be a suspense story, he could emerge as before from the subway and notice a man in a faded windbreaker, and realize he saw the same man at lunch, then again when he left a bookstore. Now here he is again, all the way into the East Village. Following him? Coincidence? He could duck into the bar to calm himself, and sit watching the scene outside, trying to locate the man again, or trying to convince himself that it is simple coincidence.

If the story is going to involve magic, give us a suggestion of that early. Leroy emerges and sniffs the air, and realizes he hasn't smelled that peculiar odor for several years, not since Mayla, his ex, took off. It smells like a superheated wire, or the air after a lightning strike, or an overheated small motor. He grew up with that smell permeating his house. The smell of magic. He hated that smell then, and he hates and dreads it now. He hurries into the bar, where he is reassured by the smell of sweat, spilled beer, and so on.

A different kind of story would follow the next example. Leroy is clutching six perfect rosebuds, an extravagance, but a necessary one. He is watching others on the subway: a teenage couple swaying into each other with the motion, an older couple holding hands, two lovely young women with arms linked. On the street, walking home, he sees his own beloved standing with a man; she takes his face in her hands and kisses him, and Leroy runs into the bar, where he is carded. He leaves the rosebuds on the counter when he leaves, one rosebud for each month he has been married.

In every case, there is a way to indicate what kind of story will follow, and although we don't know specifically what it is about, there will be enough that the question won't arise.

Leroy won't simply meander around on his way home. And in each one we will know something about the person the story is about. Not a lot, but enough to be interested.

Some writers apparently need to write their way into the story they want to tell, like taking a warm-up stretch before they get to the point. That's okay, if you learn to recognize how much of it you will then have to cut. Every line in the story should reverberate with character, setting, or the meaning of the story, and any lines that don't echo and reecho one or another or all of them should come out.

The samples above are much too blatant, too heavy-handed for accomplished writers who will instill the same kind of message much more subtly, so that when the story is developed, whatever happens will appear to have an inevitability that makes the reader nod. Surprise and inevitability are two goals worth working for. To achieve those goals, the writer must know from the first word what the story is about, what it means.

The first two pages of our twelve-page story should give

general hints about the meaning, and some details about the character and setting. The meaning is hinted at more in the following pages, the character developed, and the complexities of the situation explored. The meaning may not be entirely clear until the end, but everything that has gone before should point to it once it does become clear.

The climax, the high point of the story, should be between pages ten and twelve, no earlier, and the ending should follow as quickly as possible.

This sounds cut and dried, and of course no art form is ever cut and dried, but as general principles, this works in most short fiction. It is a generalized structure, the scaffolding from which to hang the details of the story, no more than that, but some sort of scaffolding is necessary.

As you develop your skill as a writer you will discover other structures and use them or modify them for your own use. And you will find that every part of a successful story has relevance to the whole of the story, and every part fits on the underlying structure.

To test this for yourself, you will need a paperback anthology, one you won't mind marking up, and a set of colored pencils. Decide beforehand what color represents character, a different color for setting, another one for plot and another for meaning. Read a short story several times until you know it thoroughly; then start at the beginning and underline with one of your pencils everything that is about the character, then setting, and so on. A very good story will have a rainbow effect from the first line, with character, setting, meaning, or plot all woven together again and again.

Supporters

From the start, Clarion had to struggle for funding. Robin ran it on a pittance, as he mentioned when he first proposed it in Milford. If we had thought that Clarion's future was secure, with a massive institution like Michigan State University behind it, with strong academic support, plus the support of the acting provost, who had become the full-time summer-schedule provost, we were mistaken. Funding crises continued for years, then returned intermittently even to the present. There is always a tension between the colleges of arts and letters, the literary approach, and popular culture, the commercial approach to creative writing. Each adherent struggles to maintain itself when there are budgetary problems, and since the Clarion workshop clearly fell under the popular culture umbrella, it was often seen as more expendable than the more academically inclined curriculum. Enthusiasm waxed and waned for Clarion depending on personalities over the years. And university budgets have suffered from a general lack of funding support for a much longer time. There is a perennial shortage for programs that have to compete for the same limited dollars.

There were fund-raisers for Clarion from its earliest days to the present—auctions, articles such as mugs and T-shirts for sale, booths at conventions, anthologies. Over the years, during our two weeks, we had many meetings to try to find solutions to the funding problem, many dinners with various people in power. We knew our role at those dinners: we were to explain over and over why Clarion was important. The students were establishing themselves as writers; they were exploring the implications of science and technology, winning awards. Some were teaching at universities here and there, using the methods and techniques they had learned as students at Clarion. Some were editors who demanded a high standard and literary quality writing. Others were writing meaningful television programs, writing for the movies. The university was becoming known as the host for the workshop and respected as such. Many renowned scientists admitted that their interest in pursuing a career in science arose from their early reading of science fiction. Many of them remained fans.

The university dinners were interminable, and while the students no doubt were a bit envious, believing that we were being well wined and dined, we knew that every hour spent that way was an hour in which we were not reading, were not interacting with students, were not preparing for the following day. And all those hours would have to be made up later.

There was the ever-present problem with the dorm managers, who universally did not want the Clarion group in their buildings. The students ranged in age from late teens to middle-aged and beyond. The oldest one we had was sixty-four. The median age over the years was late twenty-something, to early thirty-something. They came from every possible background, slums to suburbs, ghettos to high-rise apartments, poverty to affluence, and they did not appreciate the awful cafeteria food, and mentioned it frequently, sometimes in loud voices. They did not like the male–female segregation; they were a cohesive group, constantly sharing ideas, encouraging one another, talking at all hours. Over the years, we had lawyers, journalists, teachers—some who had never been out of academia—laborers, housewives, mathematicians, and a surgeon among the students. They certainly were not typical college students, accepting curfews, or other dorm rules more suitable for undergraduates than for adults. Although at times, watching them racing around with squirt guns, or dodging superballs or Frisbees, or climbing the fence to get to the swimming pool after closing hours, it was hard to remember that most of them truly were adults.

Many of the students had made tremendous sacrifices in order to attend the workshop. One man sold every possession he owned to raise the money. Others borrowed money. They quit jobs in some cases when they could not get time off. They left lovers, spouses, children, and other family members for six weeks. What they all shared was the same passion to become writers. They were under self-imposed pressure from the start, and with such tension always at a high pitch, they had little patience for what they regarded as petty rules.

Of course, they went too far on occasion, as when a water gun fight escalated and someone used a fire hose as a weapon. Clarion never returned to that dorm. Or when George Alec Effinger stood on a balcony on the seventh floor along with others and yelled, "Jump! Jump!" at a few Clarionites approaching the building. The dorm manager was livid; he wanted them out then and there. Didn't they know you don't yell *jump* any more than you yell *fire* in a theater? I don't think he ever really got it that the people being urged to jump were on the ground.

Vegetarians had it especially hard. We had known Paul Novitsky before, a tall, slender young man. When we arrived for week five, he appeared skeletal. One woman, another vegetarian, became so frustrated and hungry that she screamed at a cafeteria worker, "Eat death, bitch! Bring me some lettuce!"

They were out of salads that day. Clarion was not allowed back in that dorm again, either.

However they worked it, Glenn or Lenny always found another dorm manager who was willing to try the group, and one by one, we wore out our welcome all over the campus until finally we arrived at Owens Hall, a graduate residential dorm where all the students were housed on the same floor, even in the same wing. Van Hoosen Hall, with spacious meeting rooms, where the workshops were held, was across a small parking lot, and adjoining it was a complex of motel-like apartments, two stories, in a U-shaped formation with a big courtyard complete with picnic tables and grills, raccoons and black squirrels. The writers-in-residence were housed there. The units were fenced off, locked at night, secure; the residents had keys. Behind the apartment complex was a wooded area next to the sluggish brown river. It was the best housing we had ever had.

Each apartment had a living room, kitchen space, bath, and bedroom, ideal after years in dorm rooms, or in the tiny cramped apartments of the floor monitors or TAs.

For many years, the summer budget was not approved until spring of the current year, and that raised its own difficulties. Since the students had to give up six weeks of summer, they needed time to prepare, to make financial and other arrangements. It could not be a spur-of-the-moment decision. Also, it was hard to engage the visiting lecturers, the professional writers, at such a late date. Most of us plan a year in advance, and by spring, most summers are already mapped out. It also meant that the workload in the spring for the director was a significant burden. The applications were coming, stories had to be read, evaluated, decisions made, on top of the regular academic load ever present that late in the year: final student papers to read and grade.

Damon and I had long suspected that academics looked

for things in the applicants' stories that didn't concern us overly, and we suspected that our choices for students might be different from theirs. We suggested tentatively that we would be willing, and even eager, to help with the selection process. Our offer was accepted without hesitation. After that we became a committee of three: Damon, I, and the director. I made a point after that to tell the students that we were part of the committee, that we had already passed judgment on them, and if we were hard on them in the workshop, they should keep in mind that we had approved of them to start with.

Early on, Glenn and Lenny recognized the need for a larger pool of directors. Glenn was working on a project that would take years to complete—a comprehensive index of English-language short stories—and Lenny had his own projects and also a sabbatical coming up. By cajolery, bribery, or possibly simple magic, they induced others to try out as directors. Some of the other professors repeated more than once, but most of them dropped out again. Albert (Bud) Drake was heroic in serving four times. I remember sitting on a counter with him, Glenn, and Damon, to keep our feet above the rising water level as the students had a blast at a going-away party at Bud's house.

He had a philosophical smile through it all. David Wright was another newcomer who persevered. And there was M. Teresa Tavormina—Tess—and what a treasure she turned out to be.

Tess's specialities were math and science, and she taught a class in writing for science majors. She had written an article on science fiction and was a natural to recruit for the workshop. She was also a brilliant medievalist scholar who took to Clarion instantly. One of her regular students who attended Clarion that summer told me that he was shocked speechless when he saw his revered teacher soaked to the skin, tearing out after another student with a water gun in her hand.

Tess proved invaluable as the hostess and organizer for a fund-raiser that took Harlan Ellison to East Lansing in 1981 to speak to and entertain a large, paying audience. His driving terrified her, she confessed, but the fund-raiser was successful. She proved to be a marvelous critic and a great director-administrator for the workshop.

The other newcomer who stayed was Mary Sheridan, the Angel of Clarion. She was administrative assistant to the dean of Lyman Briggs at the time, and she took on the duties of being the assistant to various Clarion directors, without additional pay at first, in addition to her full-time job. Year by year, with a fluctuating appointment to Clarion duties that eventually started at 10 percent, grew to 50 percent, and was later reduced again to 25 percent of her salary, she has provided the continuity the workshop needs to function. She manages the student orientation, meal tickets, housing chores, parking passes, is on hand for emergencies, corresponds with applicants ahead of the workshop, and generally is the Jill of all trades. I don't know how the workshop functioned without her in the beginning.

The workshop atmosphere was not suitable for some of the students for various reasons. It was always under high pressure, and it made little difference if most of that pressure was generated by the students themselves. It was there. Some people deal well with stress, others suffer. Lucius Shepherd aptly called it boot camp for writers. We were trying to cram years of trial and error into six weeks. Bob Morales, from Brooklyn, could not tolerate the quiet of a summer campus largely deserted. He solved his problem by going to town, finding a bench by the high-volume traffic on the main street where he could write in a notebook. He has become a well-respected writer who still prefers New York to a more bucolic existence.

Some of the younger students who had always been stars in their schools found themselves surrounded by others equally talented, and felt diminished. Homesickness overcame a few every year. One man, newly married, stopped writing midway through the workshop, and by the time we arrived, he had stopped sleeping and eating. We told him to go home and mail us stories. And now and then there was someone who rejected any criticism at all. A few always decided they didn't want to become writers. There are no guarantees of success. No one finishes the workshop, hangs up a shingle, and prepares to meet clients or patients. Or editors. For those who require more security than freelance writing ever provides, it was liberating to accept that there were many other things they could do instead of gambling on a writing career. We thought that was a valuable lesson to learn in six weeks instead of after years of frustration and worry.

It was always a disappointment for the students when a greatly admired writer proved to be an ineffective teacher. It's true that not everyone is suitable for the role of teacher, but the students felt betrayed when it happened. We were not there when other teachers were, so nothing we heard was firsthand, but the students told us many things over the course of our two weeks. They were especially bitter about anyone who refused to criticize anything. They are astute; they knew that if they were wonderful writers, they would be out there publishing, and while they glowed if praised, they wanted the truth about what was not working for them. One teacher wanted to reorganize the workshop protocol to suit his own needs, and they rebelled. If it isn't broken, don't fix it, was their anarchic reaction. And they talked among themselves, reported whatever the teachers said in private conferences, compared notes. They were outraged when a teacher told three different students they were the best in the workshop, their stories the best.

Some students attended specifically to study under one or another teacher. One young woman told us she had wanted to write stories just like so-and-so's, and that teacher had not liked her work. She was crushed. We tried to console her. You can't be just like so-and-so, or like anyone else. That niche is already taken. You have to find your own niche. The choice is to become a second rate so-and-so, or a first-rate you.

Those six weeks proved to be life-changing for a number of students. Relationships failed, marriages failed, new friendships formed that endured through the years. New pairings, new marriages. The students formed bonds that were firm and fixed for the rest of their lives in many cases. I was bemused one evening when three women who had been to Clarion were in my living room comparing experiences. One was saying, "Remember when…" and proceeded to relate a story; the other two nodded enthusiastically. Although they had attended three different years, they made up part of the larger community of Clarionites. I have no doubt they all remembered many of the same experiences.

During the early years, as a strong support group formed at Michigan State, it was joined by David Wright. David is a dynamo. He had dual appointments then and may well have three by now. His specialty is the history of science; he was on the ethics committee overseeing science experiments; he was involved with the National Endowment for the Humanities; he taught; he was assistant to the president, and probably did many other things I never heard about. And he took on Clarion as if born to it. Skeptical, verging on cynical, he is outspoken and very funny. One night we were in one of the power groups entering a restaurant when we met him and a visiting mathematician. In a carrying voice David called out, "Time to squeeze blood from the turnips?"

How Damon and I became regulars was a mystery then,

and remains a mystery now. More than once we suggested that there were many other writers who would be fine for the last two weeks, but they kept inviting us back, and we were more than happy to return.

Delegations and Confrontations

On occasion we made the students angry, sometimes furious enough to form a delegation to protest. Frequently our ongoing battle with trivia was the cause of their fury. We read every word they wrote at Clarion in addition to their submission stories, and over and over we encountered stories too trivial to discuss. We had arrived at Clarion one year with a list of stories we forbade them to pursue. We explained each item on the list and said don't do it again.

First was the Poor Me story: *Mother hates me, Father hates me, brother, sister, teachers... Also I'm ugly and I can't get laid.*

Enough, we said. No one who asks for pity gets it. Save it for your shrink, someone who gets paid to hear your complaints. Reading is a voluntary act, and no one wants to hear a litany of whines. A dead-end, go-nowhere story. No more.

Next, the obverse: *I'm wonderful. After I slayed the dragon and rescued the damsel, I took on and destroyed the enemy and taught the inhabitants how to do everything. I solved the problems, found the treasure, was the object of every girl's desire...* Enough.

Save your adolescent wish-fulfillment fantasies for the shrink. No one likes a braggart.

The Gotcha! story: *Ha, ha, you just read three thousand words about a bug, or a cloud, or a rock, or some other insensate creature or object.*

What's the point? To prove how clever you are? A deceived reader will reject both the story and the writer. You have to play fair and be honest, or take up politics.

Anecdotes. These are the amusing or intriguing little things to mention at a dinner or cocktail party. They have no meaning outside of the small incident itself. Although they can be incorporated into a story through a character, they don't substitute for story.

The Fantasy Lover story: The lover is a dream image, a succubus or incubus, a spirit, a ghost, someone who is great in bed, then disappears. The Fantasy Lover doesn't wash dishes, leave dirty socks on the floor, go shopping, get headaches, complain… More wish fulfillment that goes nowhere. Get a live-in companion and get a life.

Travelogue, or what I did last summer. Write an article. Memoirs don't work as short stories unless and until they are fictionalized, and they never seemed to be.

No Problem. But it gets solved! Dick and Jane can't decide between the mountains or the coast for a vacation. They both like either one. They go to the coast. The Non-Problem is solved. Or the decision involves a pink or blue dress. Or chocolate or vanilla ice cream. Okay, I simplified a little, but finally the core of the story was a non-problem that was solved.

Drug Trips or Dreams. Then I woke up. Why bother? Nothing is real here; it's vaporware before there was a name for it. We got more tired of drug trip stories than we could bear, and in the end they were all the same with variations of details.

Fan Fiction. Nothing is more boring than *Star Trek* done in three thousand words with the characters given new names, or *Lord of the Rings*, or *Star Wars*. Save it for a fanzine, for someone who cares. Few editors do, and fewer readers who are not addicted to that particular show or novel. Amateurish and juvenile. No more.

Incomprehensible stories, deliberately made so by arcane knowledge and language, obfuscation, or neologisms that are indecipherable. No footnotes are allowed in short fiction, no glossary. No one wants to read a short story that requires a good dictionary or a university degree in one or another of the arts or sciences. If there's no meaning to be found, it's a dead-end, trivial story, regardless of how profound the writer judges it to be.

You must help me! No. No one must help someone else, although people often do. But it is not story material. The helper too often turns out to be an observer, and we want to read about the person directly involved, not someone implored to help, who is then free to go back to whatever she was doing in the first place.

So they sent a delegation of protest. One of the women wailed, "But there's nothing left to write about!" We could commiserate, but not relent. No more finger exercise, typing practice, filling pages just to be doing something. It can be habit forming. You don't want to train yourself to write trivia, and that's what could happen. Every time a trivial story gets treated seriously, you're strengthening the synapse that will feed you another just as trivial. It has to stop here and now. If there's nothing to write about, possibly you've chosen the wrong career. They went on strike. We met as usual; no stories had been turned in. We lectured a bit, then sent them away to write. We knew there was always a slump along about the fourth or fifth week when exhaustion had reached a peak. Then stories began to show up again, and they were real stories.

Another protest by the group as a whole came about when one of the men turned in a very long story, ten thousand words or more, that involved a lot of fighting. One battle after another fought and won by our hero, on and on and on. The students loved it, called it exciting, and we said no. It was static. Nothing happened. That met with shocked disbelief. Ten thousand words of exciting battle scenes! When they came to protest, we said much of the same that we had said in class. The hero was a man doing his job, which was to fight. He was the same at the end of the story as at the beginning, and his battles were the same basically, with cosmetic differences. If the student continued in that vein for another hundred thousand words, it would still be static. Something has to change, either in the character, in the situation, or in the reader.

He could have made it a story with a little more thought. If the warrior had done some soul searching, had come to realize how futile the endless battles were, if he had questioned his role in the ongoing death and destruction, and then did something to change, it could have been a story, not just a job description.

One year Carol Emshwiller preceded our weeks, and she stayed over for the weekend to finish things with the students and to visit with us. Algis Budrys also came for a visit that weekend, and it happened that four stories were turned in for Monday. We all read them, and Damon and I invited Carol and AJ to sit in on the workshop on Monday. We were all gloomy over the large amount of trivia the students were turning out, and we decided that a little shock treatment was in order.

The stories were pure trivia, each and every one of them. The four of us took a story apiece, and at the workshop on Monday after each story had made the rounds with the students trying to be helpful, making suggestions how to fix this or that, one by one the lecturers said there was nothing to discuss. The stories were too frivolous and trivial for comment, then passed.

We lectured on trivia and sent them away with orders to write meaningful stories. Carol and AJ departed, and that afternoon a delegation came to protest. We couldn't treat them like that, it wasn't fair, they had worked hard on those stories. The others had worked at reading them, preparing critiques, trying to be helpful. We held our ground. You could work hard at sweeping the beach clean, too, but in the end it wouldn't matter.

Another year a different kind of situation arose. A student turned in a story that hardly anyone in the group liked or understood, one that Damon and I praised. We both had points to make about the prose, but the story itself was fine. We never knew what the other teachers had stressed before our arrival, but I suspected that year that plotting had been a strong point more than once. The story in question was unplotted, a very strong story of revelation, with no discernible beginning, middle, or end—just a powerful moment of truth. If you don't grasp that moment of truth, fail to understand its significance, the story appears to fail. The class as a whole judged it a dismal failure, and even the few who got something out of it agreed that it needed more plot. We defended it vigorously. I explained it a bit, and we moved on. That afternoon, the delegation arrived.

It wasn't fair, they said. They were told to do this, do that, and then someone broke all the rules and we approved. We were biased, or the rules didn't mean anything after all, and so on.

Rules exist for good reasons, and in any art form, the beginner must learn them and understand what they are for, then follow them for quite a while. A visual artist, pianist, dancer, fiction writer—all beginning artists are in the same boat here: learn the rules, understand them, follow them. It's called an apprenticeship. A mediocre artist never stops following the rules, slavishly follows guidelines, and seldom rises above mediocrity. An accomplished artist has internalized the rules to the point where they don't have to be consciously considered. After you've put in the time to learn to swim, you never stop to think, *Now I move my arm, kick, raise my head, breathe.* You just do it. The accomplished artist knows what the rules mean, how to use them, dodge them, ignore them, or break them. This may be a wholly unconscious process of assimilation, one never articulated, but it has taken place.

One of Carol Emshwiller's students told me that he asked her if she outlined, made notes, did all the preliminary work he was told to do, and she said, "No. I just plunge in." She added swiftly, "But *you* have to."

Exactly. There are rules, and there is technique, and once the rules are understood, and technique mastered, you can do just about anything you want with words and no one will object.

It also happens to every writer I know that sometimes a story is a gift; it arrives in consciousness whole and complete, and demands to be written. It can happen to a beginning writer as well as an old pro. When it happens, yield, write it. The student whose story we praised said that was what had happened to him. The story was just there. He was not deliberately setting out to break any rules, or do anything extraordinary; he had been given a gift and used it.

We also pointed out that a story of revelation generally doesn't involve any real plotting. The reader comes to understand something new when the story is finished even if the character and the situation are unchanged.

Every year we had some students who were bewildered by unplotted stories. Some went so far as to say they were not stories at all. Real stories always had a beginning, a middle, and an identifiable end. They came to Clarion believing that, and they left believing it. I felt sorry for them.

Not all the protests were group efforts. Now and again a single student objected strongly to something or other. I noticed that one man never had a word to say about any woman's story that was being critiqued. I asked several women if he had critiqued their stories, and they said no. In fact, he had claimed in the dorm that he never read anything written by a woman. I took him aside and asked him if it was true, and he said yes. Women didn't have anything to say that he found interesting. Well, I said, I won't critique you again until you have read a few of my stories. He said he didn't have any, and I told him to go find some. I knew that some of my collections were floating around in the dorm.

A day or two later, his story came up, and when it was my turn, I passed. He looked stunned, and after class that day, he followed me out and demanded that I critique his work. He said, "You were hired to teach us, and you have to do it." I said, "So fire me." He was taken aback, and I left him standing where he was and went on to our apartment. He submitted another story, and I passed again without explanation. The next day, he came to tell me he had read one entire collection of mine overnight, and he was midway through a second one. He also said the stories were not like anything he had expected. That was more than I had required of him. After that he did his job the same as everyone else, and so did I.

A different and more difficult situation arose one year. The student involved was a creative writing teacher at the university level, and he was a very gifted writer. Word drifted back to us, the way it inevitably did, that he was undercutting most of our workshop critiques, telling students we were simply wrong, misguided, jaded, biased or prejudiced, or something else. After having their work criticized in the workshop, many of them were turning to him, the benign uncle, for consolation and soothing. And they were repeating their previous mistakes. We asked him why he was doing that, and he said we were too hard, too demanding; they needed encouragement, not criticism. I asked him how many of his own students had ever gone on to become professional writers, and he admitted that none had. Case closed. We asked him to stop, but I don't think he did. He liked playing that role, and there was little we could do about it. The pat-and-praise method of teaching works for many young people, but these were adults who were going to try to make it in the very tough world of publishing, and pat and praise was not going to do much to help them succeed.

The path to a writing career is well developed and generally familiar. You write your story, correct it to the best of your ability, put it in the mail, and then spend far too many hours watching for the mailman, fully expecting a check or a contract. Months pass—six, ten, eighteen—and one day the envelope comes back with a simple rejection slip enclosed. You have no idea why your story was turned down. Editors are not teachers for new writers. Few of them have time to become mentors. They have magazines to put out month after month, and there are enough writers who have learned their craft to fill the slots. Slush piles often are measured by feet, by yards, a year's supply of unsolicited stories piled up to be considered.

What a workshop like Clarion does, and is meant to do, is make that turn-around time a matter of a day or two instead of a matter of many months. Most stories are still rejected by the professionals, but they explain why and when possible offer suggestions about how to fix them.

These beginning writers need more than just encouragement in the form of pats and praise. Many of them have been writing and submitting stories for years without any tangible encouragement from beyond their own circle of admirers. They need to know why they are not succeeding. A workshop like Clarion is where they can find out. It is hard and it is demanding, and for those who understand and accept what it can do, it is a shortcut, often of many years.

They can get pats and praises from their mothers, lovers, and spouses. What they can get at Clarion are honest evaluations of their work from professionals who know what is publishable and what isn't, most of the time, and who can offer advice that the home folk are not trained to give. So, yes, it is hard and demanding. No one ever said it would be easy.

Another time, on our first day, several of the students came to complain about a student who was submitting pieces of a trilogy, trying to get them accepted as short stories. The pieces did not stand alone and needed the entire novel to make them comprehensible. The students said they had agreed, and warned her, that if she put in more pieces of it, the entire class planned to pass, one after another, and refuse to try to critique them. She had submitted another one that was due to be critiqued the following day, and no one in the dorm had read it, or intended to read it. They just wanted us to know what was going on.

After they left, Damon and I pulled her stories from the big pile, looked them over, compared our notes about them, and agreed that they were all bits of a fantasy novel, and indeed were incomprehensible as stand-alone stories. Pieces of novels hardly ever work as separate short stories, but she persisted in submitting them at the rate of two a week. The work load for the students to keep up with the reading was always heavy, and to have to read those pieces was a burden they were no longer willing to undertake. We also suspected that the novel was already written, and she was simply extracting pieces of it to submit as stories.

We let the students discipline their own the next day as one by one they passed. When it came to Damon, he said that no one could critique a piece of a novel with any authority, and he passed, and I more or less echoed that. We also said that during the last two weeks, no one could submit a trunk story—that is, a story written before Clarion, probably already rejected by a number of editors. There were always some that showed up during Clarion, and we tried to keep them working on new material, with the idea that what they learned during the six weeks should give them an insight into why previously written stories had not been publishable.

After the workshop, we told the novelist that before she submitted anything else, she had to show it to us for our approval, and we would not allow another piece of her novel. She protested that she was trying to write short stories, and it was not fair to single her out for special prior approval.

We talked about the difference between novels and short stories, how the novel has its own rhythms and resonances, how characters who might have been developed in the early sections might appear insane if introduced in a separate piece behaving in ways that look irrational, how fantasy words that might have been explained early are meaningless without the explanation when they turn up in a separate section, that novelistic technique cannot be applied to short stories, and so on. We told her that she could harm her novel by hearing critiques directed at pieces as if they were stand-alone stories.

She stopped arguing and asked me if I would read her novel, which indeed was already written. I had to say no. There was not enough time to read a long novel, a trilogy! I don't know if she wrote anything while she attended the workshop, but I do know she wrote nothing during the last two weeks. I hope she got something from critiquing the work of others, because I am convinced that she learned nothing useful hearing critiques of her novel.

Let the Wild Rumpus Begin

The day Richard Nixon resigned, our group was gathered in a lounge, watching television. With his words there came a great whooping and yelling and applause, while in the back of the lounge, a group of Japanese business students looked on in amazement. I suspected that in Japan that was a falling-on-the-sword occurrence, not one of jubilation.

There were always others on the campus, although it seemed deserted much of the time. Business students from other countries, bankers, history students. We were surprised one day to hear a bugle out in the courtyard, and more surprised to see a group of Confederate and Union soldiers march in, followed by a group of American history students from Japan. The soldiers were in full uniform, and outside our door they proceeded to explain everything in their kits, how the muskets worked, how they attached the bayonets, how they carried the powder for them, everything. The Japanese students listened attentively and took notes.

Another time it was marching bands practicing outside the windows, complete with cute little girls twirling batons, beginning at eight in the morning. Or a huge lawn mower going full blast, emitting clouds of smoke. Or construction across the street from the workshop room. The emptiness of the campus was illusory.

One year the students organized guerrilla theater. At the cue, the dropping of a tray, people came from the kitchen, others in the cafeteria swiveled their chairs around to watch, and the play began.

One of the skits had Tarzan rush in to rescue Jane from a kidnapper. Unfortunately, or possibly purposely, Tarzan was about five feet six, the evil kidnapper about six feet one, and Jane somewhere in the middle. Tarzan floored the evildoer with a mighty blow, slung Jane over his shoulder, and staggered out with her. She pummeled his back mercilessly, screaming at him to let her go back to her true love. Later Tarzan said he thought he had a hernia.

The following week at the drop of the tray the students all stood up and sang, "Some Enchanted Evening" when Robin appeared in the doorway. Robin never faltered, never wavered, but maintained his measured pace across the dining room and took his seat. There was great applause all around.

Annis Shepherd, born in India, educated in England, and having spent time in Australia, had along the way been a Girl Scout leader, or whatever they are called in Australia. She had learned many unfamiliar songs, some of them quite bawdy, and every night she led a troupe across the courtyard to come visit us, with them all singing lustily one or another of the songs she had taught them. There were a few other people in other units that year, and one of them routinely called the dorm manager to complain. Complaint registered, our group visited, and the party tended to get noisy again, another complaint was made, and so it went. We always chased them away between ten and ten thirty, and peace and quiet was restored. The complaining graduate student was rather bitter, and I guess I can't blame her too much. She was there to do serious work, and obviously we weren't.

They liked to play a superball game in our apartment. The

rules were quite simple: the ball had to bounce off two surfaces before it struck a person or was caught, but there were always a lot of balls flying around, and no one could quite keep track of bounces. That tended to get noisy at times, too.

Summers in Michigan are brutal. It is extremely hot, the humidity is off the scale, cool air seldom flows until nearly dawn, and thunderstorms are frequent and often violent. Most summers there are tornado warnings, and now and then a tornado touches down in the area. We were with a group one night playing word games while a storm roared. The lights flickered, then went out, and of course, no one knew how serious it might be or if anyone could sound the tornado alarm with no electricity. Then the door opened, and in came George Ewing bearing gifts of candles. He had run to his car and retrieved his survival gear and made candles in less than five minutes. He said he always traveled with a complete survival kit in the trunk. I want him nearby when the apocalypse comes. We continued our game in candlelight.

Another night, Lenny knocked on our apartment door at about eleven o'clock. We had ousted the students and were getting settled down to prepare for the next day. "You have to come with me," Lenny said. Neither Damon nor I questioned him. We went. He drove us across campus, parked, and led us to the roof of a high building. The northern sky was alight with a magnificent aurora borealis. We stood for nearly an hour in silence watching the most fantastic light show I had ever seen. I was very grateful to him. I treasure the memory of that hour on the roof watching the dancing lights with two beloved companions.

The first and, I must add, only international Moops Ball Game was held at Clarion. Gary Cohn wrote the game rules, and Damon published them in *Orbit*. I can't tell you what the rules are, but they involved two pitched camps with tents, pigs roasting on spits, music, dancing, a lot of camp raids to capture fair maidens, and so on. The students did the best they could with only one afternoon to work with. In the abbreviated game, there were two teams and the object of the game was to get a small ball across the playing field and into a garbage can. But before the action started, the ball had to be blessed or cursed by wizards. Well, Damon did not need any props to play his role. With his long gray beard and long gray flowing hair, wearing sandals, he was wizard enough. Glenn had acquired a wizard's peaked hat and a cape, and the two of them met over the ball and made mysterious passes with their hands while muttering incantations. When Damon rejoined me, he was giggling madly. Glenn had been cursing in pig latin.

I was the referee, complete with a big whistle, and the power went right to my head. I raced back and forth, whistling people off the field rather randomly, I'm afraid. One side cheated by having their player sit on the garbage can, and I whistled him off several times, but he always sneaked back.

Winded, I stopped to catch my breath, and another group of Japanese students approached me. One of them asked what the rules were. I said quite honestly that I didn't know. I was making them up as I went.

I've always wondered what impression of American university life foreign students carried back home after coming in contact with the Clarion group.

We were a little late in arriving at David Wright's country house for a party one evening. We found the students sitting in a circle on the floor, each one busily massaging the back of another. They also did foot massages and I got one, too.

There was always a final going-away party, and we had award ceremonies many times. One year it was Nebulettes. Damon and I bought some rocks, scrounged others from planter boxes, and made up the awards list. A prize for the most creative spelling.

Prize for the most original "said-bookisms." For instance, "'You can't stop me,' he galloped away." A prize for the most grotesque misuse of technology. And so on. Another year we handed out licenses. We had sent the list of students and their pictures to our son, Jon, and he and a friend made them and mailed them to us. Each one is laminated, with official seals, and they looked very real, quite authentic. Mine reads:

UNITED STATES OF AMERICA
Artistic License
** Federal Art Authority **

The part we all liked best was the one labeled Influences. Mine were G. B. Trudeau, P.I.L., #6, Sartre, "Bob," R. M. Nixon, Willie Mays. Under that was Excuses: "I lost it in the sun."

Or it might have been little toys appropriate for stories they had turned in. A racing car, a horse, a knight in armor, marbles, an alien, a spaceman...

They didn't rely on us for their fun and games, or their ceremonies, of course. At one of the parties, there was a bonfire where ritualistically they burned the manuscripts they never wanted to see again. It was a solemn rite: some of the women wore long white gowns, and there was a regular procedure that was followed as one by one each manuscript-sacrificing participant circled the fire three times with head properly bowed, hovered a minute over the flames in silent prayer, and then consigned the offending papers to the God of Writing. Afterward, there was a water gun fight.

Some of them were appalled to learn that a copy of everything they had written at Clarion ended up in the Clarion Archives. Leslie What reminded me of her story "Dial R for Rhododendron"—about a psychic plant! You'll find others there about a sentient fire that laughs merrily as it consumes a house; about talking stones, phantom lovers, "what I did last summer," mystery cafeteria meat, Adam and Eve, the sun going nova, children saving the universe, werewolves, and even a were-guinea pig.... There they are, early stories by Pat Murphy, Vonda McIntyre, Lucius Shepard, Kim Stanley Robinson, Nina Kiriki Hoffmann, Robert Crais, Octavia Butler.... Beginners' work, yes, but such talented beginners! They sometimes burned their stories, or tore them up in disgust, or simply tossed them, but copies exist, and every year the new batch of students can't resist going to the archives to see the early stories of writers who have gone on to win prizes and establish themselves as professional, bona fide, successful writers. It gives them hope.

They made use of the mammoth swimming pool and the library. They were given a tour of the cyclotron every year, and there was a planetarium, where they were invited to submit suitable stories or scripts that could be produced. The stories were usually quite bad, but many of them gave it a try. They rented bicycles one year, and another year roller skates. There were canoes for hire, ducks to feed, meandering paths to follow throughout the campus. One year there were two gourmet cooks in the group, and every day they prepared delicious dinners, using one of the apartment kitchens in the Van Hoosen complex. It was, as were most activities, a group effort. Some of them did the shopping, the two cooks reigned, then others did cleanup. That was the best-fed Clarion group of all time.

Since Owens Hall is a graduate student resident hall, the Clarion attendees no longer were treated as freshmen who needed written permission from home to go to town or stay out past ten at night. The turbulent years were long gone, and our students were mostly indistinguishable from the others in the dorm. The food was far better than that in the undergraduate residence dorms, and in later years, an espresso machine was installed in the cafeteria to everyone's satisfaction.

In a group as diverse as they were, there was always someone who knew enough to act as adviser about any topic that came up—physics, astronomy, deep-sea diving, how to hot-wire a car—whatever it was. The first time a computer turned up, the young man who brought it had located the insert key, but not the delete key, and he assiduously added just about everything he was told was lacking in his stories without deleting a word. They made for puzzling reading. Soon after that, Michigan State provided computers, and the two or three people who were already adepts were hard-pressed to keep up with the demands for their services. They began to complain that they no longer had time to write.

When computers were still new and wondrous, some of the students liked to play with fonts, make their manuscripts stand out, look good, be works of art. Just about everyone told them to knock it off.

One year a woman brought a very small cat with her, and many of them took turns hiding it when the cleaning crew made its rounds, changing linens and vacuuming. Of course, no pets are allowed in the dorms. To my knowledge, no one suspected one had been sneaked in and maintained for six weeks.

Cliques formed, dissolved, and reformed. But for the most part, the students were all very supportive of one another, ever ready to console anyone whose story took a drubbing. And for the most part, by the time we arrived for week five, they had become both quite good and honest at critiques.

There was no dinner service on Sunday nights, and usually a large group gathered and headed out for fast food somewhere. We were not enthusiastic about those dinners, since the places the students liked always seemed to have very loud music and not very good food. One time the chosen restaurant was a Mexican place in Lansing. The waiter began to bring out the plates, holding them carefully with pot holders as if they were on fire. It turned out that the dishes were ice cold, and the food was not much warmer. But at least there was no music blaring.

So we worked, we sweated, and we played.

Who Is That Masked Man?

A woman's story had a nice dad, a nice mom, nice kids, nice neighborhood, and so on. Sticky nice everywhere. Dad's nice boss offered him a nicer job in a nicer town where they could move into a nicer neighborhood and they had to decide to move or not to move. Everyone says, do it, he does, and they move. The students liked the story; they liked all those nice people, and we said no.

Fiction is not about people doing just what they want to do, or making choices that don't make any difference. It has to matter. They have to do things they do not want to do or make choices that are hard. Or it is about people who have to struggle very hard in order to do the things they want to do. If the decision matters little to the character, or if it is a choice of accepting good fortune or not, or if it is a victory without a fight, it will not matter at all to a reader.

In the classic movie *Butch Cassidy and the Sundance Kid*, there is a marvelous scene that shows this clearly. Butch and the Kid are running away from a relentless posse. They try every trick and stratagem they know to elude them, all to no avail. The pursuers keep coming. The outlaws reach a cliff high over a river, and now the choice is really hard. They have run out of options, and their choices are to give up, or shoot it out and die. Unexpectedly, and delightfully, a third choice presents itself: They can jump into the river far below. It still is a terrible choice, made worse when the Kid yells that he can't swim. But over they go. That unexpected third option is always a wonder, always a delight to the reader.

That was an action adventure film, and you would not introduce anything that extreme into a domestic story. But in real life, people have to make difficult choices all the time. Very nice people have to make hard choices. In the above story, if it had been shown that the man or his wife had an aged parent dependent on one of them, the move begins to matter. There is a price to pay whichever way they go. The loss of honor and self-respect can be life-changing. And they have options that have to be closed off one by one. People always have options, possible ways out of a dilemma. Take the mother along. Hire a caretaker. Put her in a nursing home. Turn down the good promotion. Each option is a possible one, and each comes with a price tag, either financial or emotional. That nice family could end up destroyed, or it could work out, but either way it has become a meaningful story.

Ostensibly, the above was a plotted story: however, there was no drama, no conflict, no hard choice, no undercurrents of tension or sacrifice. All stories need characters who show more than just a whipped cream topping. What lies under that surface? That's where the story exists, if there is one.

I asked this student if she didn't know people who were not quite that nice and she said no. She was in extreme denial.

By the time a child is eight to ten years old, that child has experienced every possible human emotion: loss (a beloved pet or even a blankie), fear (tree shadows on the window, the house sounds at night), betrayal (a promise not kept, a tattle-tale friend), love (parents, friends, siblings), hatred (schoolyard bully), awe (a Christmas tree), envy (I want what my friend has), jealousy (you like him better than you like me). Go over the list of human emotions, and every one of them has been felt by a child. As adults we tend to belittle childish emotions, but they are real and deep even if transitory, and we all share them. Those childhood slings and arrows provide the bottomless well to draw upon for your characters. Face your own emotions, acknowledge them, examine them, then use them.

Students are told repeatedly by public school teachers to "write what you know." I second that. Of course, you don't know Mars, or the secrets of the universe—that's where imagination and or research enter—but what you do know are human emotions, yours. And you have to dip into them if you are going to be a successful writer of fiction.

No one characteristic exists in isolation; no one is just good or just evil. We have the whole range of emotional reactions within us, with some more dominant than others, some so thoroughly repressed that they are consciously forgotten, but they all are accessible if we'll look inward deeply and honestly.

One student wrote several stories that were all basically the same: the character did not have a problem and solved it. I can't talk about real content, because there wasn't any. His prose was fluent and easy to read, even lyrical at times, but there was no story under it. All the choices were of the chocolate-or-vanilla variety. Nothing mattered to the characters. We told him to write a story that he felt passionate about, something he felt compelled to write. He subsequently wrote a story in which an adolescent boy gradually revealed that behind a facade of willing obedience and paternal love there existed a bitter hatred for his father. It was a powerful story, not as fluent and lyrical as his others had been, but real and honest. When he realized what he had written, he was horrified and went instantly back to the inane, trivial non-stories he had been writing earlier, stories that would never be published.

Another writer produced a story with a strong scientific idea, and a "rigid scientist." The story was all idea, no character. I asked him to write a biographical sketch of the character, not only concerning his appearance and statistics, but to include his inner life, his hopes and dreams, ambitions, fears, all he could think of to make a rounded character. A few days later, he turned in the new version. The big idea was still there in the background, and the story was fine. He submitted it to an editor, and the revised story was published, his first publication.

Fiction is first and foremost about people—even big ideas are secondary. This is often disputed in the world of science fiction, but nowhere else that I know, and even in science fiction, where the character and idea are joined in a happy union, the writing at the very least competent, the story is publishable most of the time. We read to learn how real people cope with the world they inhabit, whether it's a laboratory, the suburbs, the mean streets, Mars, academia—whatever that personal world is.

It is a truism that a writer reveals the self, sometimes in full awareness, sometimes unconsciously, but that is the goal. That finally is all that any of us has to offer as writers: our own perceptions of the world, our own interpretation of our culture, our experiences in fictional terms. Just as a writer must be a people watcher, the writer must look inward for the emotion that drives people. Watch people to see the range of behavior; look inward to find the cause.

Think of the worst incident of your life, and use it. Change all the objective details, make the character the opposite sex, older or younger, in a completely different situation, but keep the emotional truth. Do it again with your happiest day. You are plumbing the depths of yourself, and of truth.

It sounds paradoxical to say that one must abandon the ego to succeed as a writer, and at the same time reveal one's self. But that is exactly how it works. Readers will seldom allow you to impose your moral, philosophical, political, or any other belief system on them in fiction. When your ego clamors for attention with sermons, soap box oratory, lessons in almost anything that you believe you know more about than anyone else, you have to banish it. Your own emotional truth is all you have to offer that is uniquely yours, and whatever you believe will creep into your fiction, expressed through the characters. Unless you provide that personal, emotional truth to a fictional character, the character will be flat and one-dimensional.

You must fictionalize your experiences, let them become the experiences of your characters. If you use your own life, your own situation, you're writing autobiography, which rarely succeeds in the context of fiction. Save it for when you grow old and famous.

How to create a character who becomes plausible enough to be believable is the problem every writer has to solve. Some writers need a complete biographical sketch in writing before they can start; others discover their characters as they write them. There is a wide spectrum of possibilities between the two extremes. I need to know when my characters were born, where they were and what they were doing at the times of historical events—the Depression, World War Two, Vietnam, whatever.

I rarely write a detailed physical description of my characters, but much prefer to let the reader become my collaborator there. One time a student questioned that, and proceeded to describe one of my characters, the color of her hair, her eyes, height and weight, everything. I asked her to show me where in the story I had mentioned those things, and later she confessed that she had not found anything like that. She had become my collaborator. A reviewer described a male character as ruggedly handsome, and went on with a few details. I had not made any such assertion and had not described him in enough detail to pick him out of a lineup. That reviewer had become my collaborator. Rejoice whenever a reader becomes a participant in telling your story; that reader has been hooked.

Other writers have a need for detailed descriptions, and that is fine as long as it works for them. But keep in mind that judgments of what is beautiful vary widely. Some people might think a bulimic super model is the epitome; others delight in the Titian lush beauty. Many women feel threatened by men over six feet tall; others search them out. A classic case illustrates this principle. There was a novel titled, *The Most Beautiful Girl in the World*. The author did not describe her, and all over the world teenage girls could identify with her. When the paperback edition came out there was a blue-eyed blond on the cover. That excluded 90 percent of the world's teenage girls.

Unless there is a good dramatic reason to describe the characters, try to let the characters within the story see one another according to their own emotional involvement.

I suggested an exercise to demonstrate this. A woman enters a restaurant where she is meeting her lover. He is passionately in love with her. Have him describe her. Have someone else present describe her, someone who hates her. Then write a third description made by someone present who is totally neutral. They should not all see the same woman the same way.

Another exercise. Using one of your own stories, write a scene that is confrontational with three people involved. It can be a scene actually written already, or one that will never be used, just so you use your own characters. First write it from the viewpoint of your protagonist. Then again from the other two viewpoints. Try to visualize your story scenes like this, and see if they change. What one person sees as reasonable behavior another might see as belligerent or hostile, or possibly insane.

Some people use the phrase "squeeze your character." Generally I say force your character into a corner and see who comes out. A raging tiger, a wimp, a whiner? Maybe no one, a person who hides behind her hands and refuses to deal with her problem. You should know the extremes of her behavior. If a previously repressed emotion becomes dominant, what will it replace? What will recede into the background and become inoperative? Something will. But before the squeeze, we have to have seen normal behavior in order to compare the change that overcomes a character in deep trouble.

People allude to their childhood landscapes or their home lives, their religion, education, various things from the past automatically. A woman from the deep South might curse the April-into-May frosts that kill her newly started tomato plants in upper New York. A person from the plains might feel claustrophobic in the canyons of New York City, or threatened by the dense northwest forests. And most people relish the foods from their childhood, whether croissants and truffles or collard greens and corn bread. If you know enough about your characters to use such allusions, you will add depth, solidity, reality.

People share and understand many fears that can become so intense, they blend into phobias: fear of heights, rats, snakes, spiders, and such. These are generally accepted as human characteristics with no further explanation needed. If your character has a fear verging on phobia to more ordinary objects, creatures, or motions, an explanation is called for. We want to know why Lady MacBeth is a compulsive hand washer, for example. Few people like the sight of blood, but even fewer faint or scream at the sight of it. We would want to know why your character reacts so violently. A train whistle in the distance might go unnoticed by most of us, but if your character becomes strained and weepy, tell us why. A melody might make one person become dreamy eyed, no questions asked. But if someone else goes into a rage or freezes in horror, that calls for an explanation. Any behavior out of the range of what most of us consider the norm needs an explanation, and unless that explanation ties in with the story, it is usually better to leave that behavior out.

Now and then a student knew enough about a character to elicit weird behavior that appeared inexplicable, and while the writer knew the entire background of the cause, the readers knew nothing of it and felt only bewilderment. What might be very evocative to the writer remains a mystery to the reader who then begins to doubt the reliability of the narrator or the character.

I'll warn you up front that the following exercise is extremely difficult, but give it a go. Try writing a page or two of dialogue with your characters without any attributions. No *he said* or *she said*, no names given, only the dialogue. Their speech patterns should vary enough to distinguish who is speaking, and speech should never sound like the narrative.

If you have ever read transcripts, you know how repetitious and redundant most speech is, how punctuated by "um" or "er," things like, "What I mean is..."

Few people talk in complete sentences in casual speech, and the closer emotionally they are to one another, the more verbal shortcuts they use. There is a saying that people who have lived together for many years no longer need to tell a joke; they can refer to it by number and get the responding laughter. Linguists say that almost half of all speech is redundant. We make our point, then rephrase it and wait for nonverbal signals to inform us if we are being understood. If no signal is forthcoming, we rephrase.

Sometime use a tape recorder in a group of four to six people who are having a casual conversation—with permission, of course. Listen to it later. You probably will hear half sentences, pauses, interruptions, abrupt changes of subjects, perhaps one voice dominating the group. Listening will give you a sense of how chaotic real dialogue can be, but you will not get the full impact because the visual cues will be missing. We read body language as well as listen to the words, and somehow—it often seems in spite of ourselves—we communicate. You have to try to capture that without all the pauses and redundancies because that becomes tedious very quickly. Speech patterns, allusions to the past, the sparing use of colloquialisms: they all work to differentiate and delineate characters.

Pay attention to the differences in the way men and women talk. She'll say something like, "I don't think that will work." He more likely would say, "That isn't going to work." There is a real difference in their language, but you have to develop an ear for it. We use a different vocabulary when we talk to intimates than when we talk to outsiders, and yet a different one when we talk to children.

Remember that words are often used to conceal rather than reveal, and body language may well convey a truer message many times. It can be extremely effective to have your character hear the words, then respond to the body language.

Where was your character a year before the story began? A month before? Supposing she survives at the end, where will she be tomorrow? Characters shouldn't be born on page one and vanish when the story ends. Even people who discover characters as they write them discover much about their pasts and possible futures.

If you can describe your character with a two- or three-word phrase, you're probably writing a stereotype. The kindly doctor, the harried housewife, the rigid scientist, the miserly banker, and so on. Think instead: a woman who has a medical practice, a man who does research as a theoretical physicist, a man who manages the local bank. It's a good practice to know who the person is before you know what the person does.

Characters have to be interesting. They don't have to be sympathetic or likeable. That seems to surprise some beginning writers who have been taught that you start with a sympathetic character. That is the most common way, but Hannibal Lecter is not someone you would invite to Sunday dinner, nor is Jack the Ripper or the Talented Mr. Ripley. But, my goodness, are they interesting! What is important is to make the reader care what happens to that character and what he does about it. Or make the reader want to know what he is going to do next and if he will get away with it.

Today, great fiction is seldom written about millionaires or royalty. It is most often written about people who at a glance would appear to be regular, everyday, common folks, like most writers. These ordinary people might become involved in extraordinary adventures, but they remain recognizable as the kind of people you might see on buses, trains, in the subway, in offices, in your own home. And great fiction reveals that there is no such thing as a common, everyday uninteresting person. They are all interesting if you learn enough about them to discover who lives behind the facade.

Few people reveal themselves in a social gathering, or even after many brief encounters with others. Behind that public, affable, polite face, there often lives someone quite different. The outgoing extrovert with the ready joke and laugh may harbor a deep inferiority complex that he doesn't dare reveal or even acknowledge. The ever-helpful, apparently altruistic person may be pleading, "Like me, accept me, tell me I'm okay." The kindly face may conceal a secret brute. The fierce, scowling one may be the one who would nurse a sick kitten to health or be there when a friend is in deep trouble. Invariably when someone is convicted of a particularly gruesome murder, others will be ready to testify that he was always kind, considerate, quiet-spoken, helpful. You have to peel away the public layers and find who exists under the skin—then you'll have a realistic character.

Often what lies behind the mask is nothing more violent than an extraordinarily rich fantasy life. The middle-aged teacher may see herself on a stage performing before thousands, living the life of a celebrity. The corporate attorney may do battle with aliens or monsters, or solve the problems of the universe, or something else far removed from reality. The mechanic may be a space explorer. If the fantasy life becomes too overwhelming, too compelling, the character may find himself living that life and leaving the mundane, and he may be sinking into neurosis, or even a deepening psychosis. The banker who fantasizes himself as a Casanova may start stalking a beautiful woman. The teacher may run up enormous debt to provide a proper setting for the celebrity she wants to be. As these characters become more obsessed, they often become more interesting. Most readers are fascinated by obsessed characters.

Or the fantasy life could just bob along gently and make day-to-day existence more bearable. If that's the secret self, let us see it, and many of the readers will nod and identify with that character.

In fiction as in life, we don't start by seeing that inner self. We see the helpful grocery clerk, patient and smiling, or the staid, solid banker, or the zany office clown. We have no way of knowing how any of them will react when subjected to intolerable pressure. The phrase "going postal" has entered the vernacular; we all know what that means. It is the writer's task to show the change, however slight or major it may be, and its cause.

Real people can't survive in a vacuum. Your character is

someplace, a place that is real, a place that influences her or is influenced by her or both. It is not informative to say something like, "When she heard the footsteps drawing closer, she raced around the corner and ducked behind a wall." Corner of what? City street? Alley? Hospital corridor? Apartment building? Cornfield? What kind of wall? Stone, brick, wood, dirt, metal, something else altogether? If I have to form my own image of that corner and that wall without your guidance and on the next page or later you mention that she is in a spaceship, or on Mars, or in a medieval village, probably I'll turn to the next story. Many, perhaps even most, readers form images as they read, as you want them to do, and if those images are nullified later, readers tend to lose patience. *Why didn't you tell me that before?* would be the complaint if they bothered to register one.

What is even more probable is that no paying customer will ever see that passage because it will go into the self-addressed stamped envelope and sent on its way back to the writer.

So, know your character, the hidden self as well as the public self, put that character in a real place, and then get on with the story. It sounds so simple: one, two, three. For many inexperienced writers, it proves to be quite elusive and difficult.

Where Am I?

One of the women wrote a story in which everyone lived within a walled community, a compound encircled by a wall too high to see over. The story had a surreal quality in spite of fairly realistic action. I asked her what lay behind the wall, and she didn't know. I asked if anyone in the community knew, and she said it had not come up in the story and she had not thought about it. That explained the surreality.

Were the inhabitants placed there? Can they leave? Is the wall to keep them in, or to keep an enemy out? Has no one ever left and returned? Is the community absolutely self-sustaining? No supplies coming in, no exports going out? Each question opens a fan of possibilities, too many for one short story.

The writer has to know what lies beyond the wall and has to give the readers enough direct instructions or else imply enough through the characters' behavior for the readers to be able to piece it together.

Think of a story as existing at the peak of a high pyramid, with the pyramid foundation anchored in bedrock in a real world. A world exists in which the pyramid is appropriate. The structure itself is the general setting for the story, with a particular culture and a level of civilization and technology that is appropriate for the story. The peak is the immediate setting where the actions of the story take place. They are all necessary. Although the peak is the focus of a short story, the foundation and the world have to be implied one way or another.

The background, the world with its diversity of creatures and cultures, the period of time in which the story takes place, and the general setting are all necessary ingredients to establish the reality of the immediate setting. The immediate setting can not float in a void.

Setting, world, and culture are so intricately wed to character that it is nearly impossible to talk about one without the other. We are affected by our world and our setting, and we have an effect, however infinitesimal, on it.

Every living creature shares the trait of curiosity, and the higher the level of intelligence and imagination, the greater the curiosity, until in humans it becomes a powerful drive. We have to know what lies beyond the wall, what treasures or terrors exist in the deepest sea trenches, what is under the frozen poles, what is at the edge of the ocean, over the mountain, in the darkest forests. What is on the dark side of the moon, on Mars, beyond Jupiter? We are driven to learn what is out there.

I asked that same woman if she had peeked over the wall while thinking of the story and she said she never visualized stories at all. While I cannot imagine writing without an active visual imagination, apparently many writers do it that way. I came up with a simple test for the students to determine how active their own visual imaginations were.

Close your eyes, and then imagine someone walking up stairs. That's it. I gave them only a second or two; then I told them to open their eyes and jot down what they had seen, if anything. Most of them wrote something, but a surprising number of them had nothing to write yet. For some people, the images flow more rapidly than they can cope with: a woman in an evening dress going up a regal staircase in a grand ballroom, a boy scurrying up a fire escape, someone plodding up narrow tenement stairs that are badly stained and smelly, a man walking up a broad outdoor staircase to an official building. Those were real images, all of them, and as that group wrote, it became obvious that each detail furnished others. Think of those writers as visualizers.

For those with nothing to write yet, a structure of some sort had to be built for the staircase, then a person created and put on it; word-by-word construction had to take place. Those writers are constructionists.

For those who visualize as they write, it would seem very simple to describe what they have seen through the mind's eye, but it does not always happen this readily. Sometimes if the mental images are very sharp and strong, the slightest clue will be sufficient for the writer to furnish the rest of the description mentally, but that small hint may not evoke the same vision for the reader. The writer who visualizes must learn to sift through a plethora of material, to pick and choose specific details that will allow the reader to form approximately the same picture that is in the writer's mind. It will never be exactly the same, but it should be as close as possible in order for the reader to follow the action of the story.

For those who rely on logic and words to convey what is necessary for the story, there falls the chore of constructing the setting, then deciding what should reasonably be included, and they often forget to include the general setting and the implied world. Also, surprisingly, they sometimes overwrite, describe too much in too much detail, as if after going to all that work, they are reluctant to discard a single effort. Often they fall back on clichés because that's the easiest way to get on with the story.

The two ways of arriving at the setting as done by constructionists or visualizers usually will differ widely. A simple scenario might illustrate this. A woman emerges from the subway and has several blocks to walk home to a high-rise tenement, where she lives on the fourth floor. She is carrying two large bags of groceries from the store where she is a cashier. She's tired and angry because her shiftless boyfriend didn't meet her at the subway to help carry things.

A constructionist might take a paragraph or two to describe the awful street—a store window boarded up, broken glass strewn on the fractured sidewalk, the smells, traffic noises, and so on—and then start creating a woman trudging along. We would get the picture, but it would not be very economical.

A better technique might be to construct the street and the woman, and then merge the two instead of introducing them separately. The woman is in a definite place from the start. It would be nearly impossible to visualize her otherwise. In the end, it should not matter which method is used; the result should be much the same.

In either method we could see her coming from the subway, and we know what she experiences: the bags she is carrying limit her vision below, but she can feel broken glass crunching underfoot, she might try not to breathe deeply the air thick with exhaust fumes, feel nauseated by the smell of garlic, onions, and chili peppers in hot oil; her fatigue making her less careful than she would be otherwise, she might twist her ankle slightly on the crevice created by the fractured sidewalk. Her anger would probably grow step by step as she walks.

We would get the same picture in both instances, but in the latter we would get something else as well, a character reacting to her world, being affected by it with her anger growing. And every sensory detail would help define the character: she feels the glass underfoot, she smells the garlic and oil, she hears the traffic noises, she sees boarded-up windows. No longer is it the author telling us what we should know to understand the story; now it is the character experiencing her world.

What she smells clues us to her neighbors, probably Hispanic, and suggests that she is not Hispanic, since the odor is disagreeable to her. The disrepair of the sidewalk tells a lot about the general setting; traffic places it in the here and now. A constructionist might still have to create each component separately, but they can then be linked. It is good technique anytime you can combine character with setting.

Another useful technique is cinematic, with a sweeping overview, then a narrowing of the focus until we are with the character. Imagine a broad overview of mountains, white tops dazzling in the sun, the blue cloudless sky punctuated by a contrail drifting apart. In a high alpine meadow, red columbines are coming into bloom. A stream races, gray with snowmelt, and a man in hip boots stands fly-fishing in the water. On shore, next to a backpack and within reach, is an assault rifle.

This kind of opening places us in a real world. We can fill in the rest. Contrail, assault rifle, backpack, hip boots tell a lot about the culture and period, and even a bit about the man, and our curiosity is aroused. Why an assault rifle on a fishing trip?

One sharp, correct detail can take the place of a paragraph of generalities. That one detail can make the world real so we don't feel we're adrift in a void.

I usually draw house plans for the buildings I write about. I need to know where the doors are, where the halls are, and where they lead to. I often use real city or county maps and alter them to suit my own purposes. Or I draw my own. I need to know how long it would take to get from here to there, what kind of terrain lies between point A and point B. Also, I feel very free to clear an entire area and build my own community, my own woods or city streets, with the kinds of buildings, shops, or whatever else my story needs. I may use a real highway, a street on a city map, and then add another one that isn't on the map for my own purposes. That street I just invented doesn't exist in your real world, but I make it as real as possible in my fictional world, and unless you look for it and fail to find it, not only should you never know it is my invention, you should not even ask. Other writers clear the space also and refurnish it, and that's one of the reasons why you can't use anyone else's fiction for your own research in any way. A published writer may have a hundred or more details of the setting to work with, some inventions, others based on the real world. She can pick and choose from a wealth of information what she needs, and end up using no more than ten details. If you use that writer's details for your own setting, you start with ten to pick from, and since you can't use them all or you could be guilty of plagiarism, you might end up using one or two details, and the ones you choose could well be the invention of the original writer. One setting will be rich and plausible; the second one will be flat and unconvincing.

The city I see is not the same one you might see. One who knows plants can go into the country and return with a basket of edible greens where someone else sees only unkempt weeds. We all have different areas of interest, a different focus even when we're looking at the same landscape, or at the same person.

You must do whatever research is necessary for your story, and primary sources are always the first choice. If you are writing about a museum, visit a few, pay attention to the lighting, the placement of art, and so on. Read up on museums. With the Internet available to almost everyone, research has become so accessible that there is no excuse for anyone not to make use of it. Fiction should never be a primary source for your research. Whatever that published writer learned has been filtered through that writer's needs, which are never your needs. What works well is to use enough of what's real to establish a solid core of belief, and then invent as you need to.

The Clarion Workshop is officially for writers of science fiction and fantasy short stories, but to my knowledge none of the instructors ever insisted that the students write only that. I know that we never did. Nevertheless, many of the students did write science fiction and fantasy, and most of them got into trouble almost immediately when they decided to place their action on other worlds, other planets.

One story was about a colony on a far distant planet where the settlers were struggling with fierce native beasts. We knew it was not Earth because there were three moons, the planet had a strange name with apostrophes here and there, and the creatures were named something unpronounceable.

The story elicited a great many questions. Had the writer thought of the different tidal forces? The different kinds of weather, the distance from the primary star, the different pathogens—bacteria, viruses, fungi—in the soil and air? Evidently not, because the colonists were trying to grow what looked very much like wheat with a funny name. And the fierce creatures looked suspiciously like saber-toothed tigers with scales and funny names.

James Blish put it succinctly: Don't call a rabbit a *smeerp.*

Creating a believable setting right here on our own rock is hard enough, but to create an entire planet, and then a local setting is Herculean and might well be considered more the setting for a novel than for short fiction. If the story can be told on the Siberian tundra, or in the vastness of the Brazilian forests, or in Nebraska, go there. History is replete with stories of settlers doing battle in hostile environments, and it is still going on. No one needs a whole new planet and solar system to add to that material.

Beginning science fiction or fantasy writers sometimes argue that because theirs is a work of pure imagination, they are free to invent whatever they want and need for story purposes. And I agree, up to a point, with the warning: You have to make your world consistent to make it plausible. If you are writing about an immense Saharan desert with nothing but sand dunes from horizon to horizon, you can't plant a tree to provide convenient shade.

If you are writing about a distant planet, you have to stop and think about where the strange names of plants and animals came from. Any immigrant who has had his name changed summarily by an immigration official can testify that the one in authority feels free to make whatever changes are necessary to fit an unfamiliar name into his own perception of what is acceptable in his own language. It is hard to believe that colonists on a distant planet would adopt unpronounceable names for the flora and fauna they encounter, even if they have a native population to inform them.

Place and culture are intricately bound. One student wrote a story about a Balinese sculptor who was innovative and original, and highly regarded by his own people for his creativity. However, in such a traditionalist society, those are not qualities usually appreciated. The ideal is to replace what is worn out or broken with a replica of what was there originally, so that it is impossible to tell if the object is new or hundreds of years old. The new original carvings are in hidden places, on the back side of stairs, or under overhangs where they will not be seen unless one looks carefully. Creativity is often the cause of artists leaving such a society to find a more hospitable welcome elsewhere. Some Balinese dances have not changed for thousands of years. To impose American values in such societies results in failure most of the time.

There is a travel book about two North American explorers who set out to explore part of the Amazon basin, then up to a high

Andes peak. At first food was plentiful, with game, local fruits, and other vegetation easily found along the way. As the expedition continued to the mountain, food became scarcer, and they had to cut rations, then cut them again. Up past the tree line there was no food to be found except their diminishing provisions, until by the time they reached the summit and started back down, they were very hungry, and even at the point of starving. The natives finally spied a tree that was alive with caterpillars and cocoons, and they were jubilant. They brought out a kettle and proceeded to make a stew, which they all relished as nourishing and wholesome. When the white men tried to eat it, their stomachs rebelled violently, and they were in worse condition than before. They had to be carried for miles, too weak to walk.

This is the reality of the human condition. North American natives wondered at the white men who were hungry amidst plenty: caterpillars, grasshoppers, crickets, snakes, roots... Yet students often had their colonists on distant planets eating the local foodstuffs, planting Earth crops in alien soils, without a thought about the reality of life on that planet. And most often the writers imposed American values with minor variations on any alien society they encountered.

But, they argued, humans have always explored and sent colonists to newly found lands, and the answer was that there was also a sound economic reason for that. Gold from Central and South America, furs and timber from North America and later a lucrative slave trade and cotton, spices from the Far East, control of sea lanes. Empire building. Behind every great wave of exploration and colonization, one can find a strong economic incentive. If the reason was not economic for space colonists, but simply to seed the galaxy with humans, with the technology available for such a mammoth task, why were the colonists so often so poorly equipped to deal with what they found on those distant worlds? The colonists who came to North America brought the contemporary technology of Europe with them, and unfortunately the space colonists often take that same obsolete technology with them. Why? Not only was that question seldom answered, but it was even more seldom addressed. The students just wanted to write about space and colonies.

We did not try to dissuade them from writing about other worlds, space travel, or anything else, but we did urge them to consider the reality of whatever setting they were writing about, and not substitute a Disney version or one derivative of a television series.

Whatever background and specific setting you use will be patently false unless and until every impression of it has passed through your own mind, attached itself to your own interpretation and interest. You will have to invent each setting, no matter if it is New York City, your hometown, a village in Mexico, or a distant planet. You have to invent it, or reinvent it, every time. Ask yourself repeatedly, What would it really be like? Would a newly arrived immigrant from Puerto Rico see the same New York that Woody Allen sees? How about a student from New Mexico? An Iowa farmer might regard the Great Basin as nothing but a wasteland to be filled with nuclear waste without hesitation. Those who love the high desert will see something else. Examine whatever background and setting you use through the eyes of your characters, not from an article in a national magazine or a travelogue. The landscape will change depending on who is regarding it.

Whatever setting you use, make sure it is consistent within itself and with whatever period you are writing about. If you know what lies on the other side of the wall, enough of that information will infiltrate the story so that we, the readers, will believe in the reality of your world.

What's Going On?

When someone recommends a story, the usual question you might ask is, "What's it about?"

The answer could be something like: This guy has to come up with a hundred thousand dollars by Friday. Or, someone has discovered anti-gravity. Or, a guy's car breaks down in this small village where vampires are said to exist. Or something else. That's the situation. It isn't the story. The situation is where the story begins in the reader's mind, whether or not it's where the writer began. The story happens when the situation is developed.

In the story I mentioned earlier, the very long story of endless battles, the situation is that the warrior has to fight the enemy and win one way or another; then he has to do it again, and then again. The basic situation is exactly the same throughout. Nothing was developed. It failed as story.

The situation may be of the big-idea type: What if we had anti-gravity? What if we found a cure for every illness? What if a pandemic swept the earth, leaving few survivors scattered here and there? What if the aliens came? These are big ideas with world-wide implications.

Or the situation could be on the order of, What would it be like to be ... and anything might follow: a trapeze artist? a telepath? invisible? a traveler stranded in a blizzard without food or water? lost at sea? an artist going blind?

It could be a very close and personal what-if story. What if you learned your lover was cheating on you? What if you were diagnosed with a terminal illness? What if you were the unluckiest person on earth? What if you won the lottery? What if you had three wishes guaranteed to be granted?

The possibilities for situation are endless and easy to think up. Developing them into story is the work. Any story situation can be turned into a real story. It's the soup stone, the driving force for the story. The film director Alfred Hitchcock called it the MacGuffin. One year at Clarion just before a coffee break I posed the following situation to show what I meant by story situation. Aliens have come. They are invisible and intangible, bodiless. Try to think how that could be made into a story. When we regathered, there were some suggestions about how to develop a story, but they were all meaningless. Finally Damon said, "As given, that can't be a story. The aliens have no effect on anyone, they pose no menace, they aren't after our beautiful women or our water or anything else. The only way to make it become story is to work from the aliens' point of view."

Exactly. If no one is affected, there is no story. From the point of view of the aliens, depending on why they came, what they want, if they are frustrated, or whatever, it possibly could become a story.

I think of the situation as the precipitating event. There is order, equilibrium, and no matter how chaotic or dangerous life is, if that's the status quo, that's the equilibrium. A fireman risking his life, a soldier going into battle, a deep-sea explorer going down in a submersible—whatever it is, if it is his job, something he does routinely, that's the equilibrium. Something upsets it, and it must be resolved. That "something" is the precipitating event, and now you have a situation to be developed.

One way the situation can be made into story is to develop it laterally. There is visible cause and effect. The hero acts, and there is an effect—good or bad—and he acts again, then again, until by the end of the story you have restored equilibrium or order.

Or it can be developed vertically. No one does much, possibly, there may be no visible cause and effect, but the situation is explored in more and more depth, its implications explored, and by the end, the reader has been informed of the true meaning of the situation and what it means to the characters. Meaning has been revealed or illuminated. At the end of this kind of story, the situation may be exactly as it was in the beginning, and what has changed is the reader's understanding. This story may be quiet and introspective, or it may be very active with a lot of adventures, confrontations, but the action does not have an effect on the basic situation.

Quite often a story seems to lie midway between the two methods. The situation is developed thoroughly, but the protagonist does not act until the end of the story, and you have no way of knowing exactly what that action will mean in the future. That is just another kind of plotted story with most of the real plot implied, or left to the reader to supply. The situation is changed because finally the character is going to do something about it, but the only effect is by implication.

All the approaches above are valid; no one is better than another morally, ethically, or esthetically. They all can and do produce very good fiction, or quite bad fiction. You may prefer one to another as a writer or a reader, and that's valid also. What is not valid is to say I didn't understand this story, or I don't like this kind of story—therefore, it's a bad story. Tastes in fiction vary as much as in any other area, as they should.

Some of our students resisted the idea that an unplotted story could be good, and that was a pity. Others could not bear the plotted stories they thought of as too contrived and manipulated, and that was a pity also.

Some students said they couldn't plot at all. The story got silly, or they couldn't think of a way to resolve the situation. My advice is to try telling stories to children. Don't retell stories from books; make them up. Children are a demanding audience. They insist on an identifiable situation, a problem, a solution to the problem, and a satisfying, identifiable resolution. You have to get little Timmy out of the well, get the robbers out of the house, find the secret door and escape. And you have to do it in a way that your audience would not have thought of. Surprise them. If you can hold their attention, you can plot.

I came up with an exercise I wanted everyone to try, whether they wanted to write plotted stories or not. First part: Write a sketch of a situation for a plotted story, and a possible resolution. I told them they didn't have to do more than outline an idea, no story was demanded. Dutifully they turned them in, and some were pretty good. Then I said the next step was to put aside the solution they had come up with and find another one, a bit more difficult or complicated than the first. There was some grumbling, but they went away and tried. I had one more step. Now put that resolution aside also, and come up with a third one. The grumbling turned to howls. Unfair! Unreasonable! They had already given it their best. But they did it. And in succeeding, they wrote plot outlines for possible stories. The third resolution often was one that the reader would not have expected or furnished herself. That's what a plotted story consists of.

There is a situation that is problematic, there are attempts to alleviate it or get rid of it altogether; the attempts usually fail or make it worse; there is a crisis point where all seems lost; there is the final solution that resolves the problem and changes the situation.

The intermediate steps are seldom thoroughly explored

and attempted in short fiction because there is not enough space to allow that. But they should be considered, and one by one the possible ways out, the ways that rational people would try, have to be closed off. In the case of the man who needs a large amount of money by Friday, say to pay ransom for his wife who will be killed if he doesn't meet the demands of the kidnappers, there is a desperate need to get the money. He could tap his rich uncle; uncle is climbing Mt. Everest, out of reach. He could sell his house; he has too little equity in it, and there wouldn't be enough time anyway. He could borrow; he just lost his job and has no credit. He could rob a bank, but readers already thought of that. He turns to familiar technology and prints out bogus bills that will fool the kidnappers temporarily. But that was not his first choice.

Using the simplified outline above, I can tell you what won't work. An act of God can't intervene; the kidnappers can't get zapped by lightning. The wife can't make an impossible escape and call off the whole thing. He can't win the lottery. No third party can come to the rescue. In other words, it's his problem, and he has to solve it himself. He can't show extraordinary abilities suddenly. What he does has to be consistent with what you have indicated he can do. Tell us very early that the job he lost was in high technology; he knows computers and design well enough to attempt the bogus bills.

Some of the students went on to write the stories they had outlined. Some were reproachful for my having put them through the wringer. One is still reproachful years later. Hello, J.

The big-idea story often does not come with a particular character attached. You have to find the suitable person by asking whose story it is. There has to be someone who is intimately involved. There are a number of questions to be asked and answered, in fact. The answers could lead to the protagonist.

First, is the big idea just now being discovered, or is it established and accessible? The resulting stories will be totally different. Keep in mind that no one can predict with confidence the outcome of any major innovation. No one predicted the rise of antibiotic-resistant bacteria when penicillin was hailed as a miracle drug. No one predicted urban sprawl when Henry Ford was tinkering with internal combustion machines. No one predicted the lack of a good road system in Colombia, South America, when air transport made it easier and more economical to fly over the jungles and around the mountains than to build roads.

In the instance of a cure-all drug, try to think of all the eventualities that could arise before you take another step. Immortality? Maybe not, just good health for a normal life span. A population growing rapidly as millions of lives lost to disease would now be saved and reproduce. Or would that not be an issue if we knew our own good health would continue? You would add many more questions here, but that is the idea. And you still have no character.

Then you have to turn it over and ask who would be hurt by it. The entire medical industry—pharmaceuticals, hospitals, doctors, nursing homes... You are getting closer to finding your characters: those who passionately want to develop this and possibly an extremely powerful, extremely rich group who might not want it done.

Or it could be a race between two competing groups, the way Linus Pauling and Jonas Salk raced to be first with the polio vaccine. Each group might try to sabotage or outwit the other. But it's still a group.

Narrow it down again. You don't want "the scientist" opposed by the "ruthless tycoon." Your character could have totally selfish motives: a man driven by ambition, the need to climb aboard the pedestal occupied by Pasteur and Einstein.

Or he could be selfless: someone who has watched one family member after another die of an incurable disease. He can't just be doing his job, going home to watch the ball game and have a beer, and then going to work the next day. And he can't be an uninvolved observer. He has to care deeply. It has to be a person, and this is what he is doing because he has to do it. The big idea won't vanish, but you won't write an article that is trying to pass as a work of fiction.

One of the reasons that most teachers in middle school through high school and into college courses and, regrettably, even intensive workshops teach plotting as the major story-telling method is that it is teachable, and it is learnable. There is a template, and no matter how much the story parts are scrambled in the words on paper, if the story is restored to a chronological timeline, the pattern is discernible. Parts may be skimped, or even missing, but the story follows certain guidelines; it moves from order to disorder and back to order.

Paradoxically, many (perhaps even most) very short stories do not follow that template. It is hard to fit a real plot into a story under five thousand words, but even more importantly, much short fiction is not about overcoming obstacles. It is about how people behave, who they are, how they fit into society, how technology influences their lives, how they manage or mismanage their relationships, things of personal interest.

By its nature, the unplotted story exists in a state of anarchy. There are no defining guidelines, no template, no rules to follow, only general broad principles. It is easy enough to critique such stories on the basis of success or failure, but even that is highly subjective. You dig it or you don't.

Having said that, I can give a hint of the principles. If it is a day-in-the-life-of story, the life being illuminated must be thoroughly plumbed and understood, and its essence presented in the story. Whether it's the life of a barefoot peasant or a society trend-setter, that life must be understood and explored and meaning derived from it. The peasant may have a life that a sophisticated city dweller would find intolerable, but by the end of the peasant's story she should have an understanding that she never had before about him or his life. And, of course, the writer can't reveal the meaning of this life unless and until she has thoroughly grasped it.

I'll illustrate this with a personal story. I had the opportunity to spend an afternoon in Colombia with a woman of great wealth who was about my age, with children about the ages of my own. She was a writer who had had considerable success in her own country. She had a house full of servants, a driver, a gardener, and wanted for nothing material. At a glance, her life presented an enviable dream. Late in the day, she confided she would trade it all for my life. Shabby and impoverished in comparison to her, I was taken aback by her sincere confession. I had personal freedom she explained. I could go to New York and meet my editor or agent for lunch. I could travel to a university to lecture, or have a weekend holiday with other writers or friends. I was not bound by my culture the way she was. She felt impoverished and envious of me.

I came away from that meeting with an insight I had not had before. And that's the kind of insight that is needed to fulfill the demands of an unplotted story about a human life. Who is behind the mask? What fears, longings, desires, what passions lie there? That woman's life is not going to change; she is a captive of her own culture, but my perception of her changed.

If you want a story about a different society, a post-holocaust society, for example, first you have to put yourself there for a time. What would it really be like? You have to have imagined it thoroughly. How many amenities that we take for granted would be missing? How would anyone cope with the fear that would inevitably arise? How would society organize itself politically? Where would the food come from? On and on. The second half of this problem is to make all the differences appear to be routine, just as we may find it routine to encounter gridlock on the freeway.

A student wrote a story about a mother instructing her daughter about household chores, how to do this, how to do that, and at first it appeared quite trivial, but then the mother pricked her finger with her needle, and she and the daughter watched the blood drops well up and drop, and there came the moment of truth of the story. It was about mortality. The mother had passed on her genes, and now she was passing on her wisdom and knowledge. Many of the students did not understand it and judged it another failure. I thought it was a fine story.

Stories like these must have that moment of truth that reveals the meaning of the story. And the revelation must be something the reader might never have considered before in such a context.

There are stories that apparently are about one thing, but then turn into something else. Max is a brilliant scientist, fifty-something, a loner, who talks to himself and hardly anyone else. He is shy and inarticulate. He has come up with many lucrative discoveries for his company. His superiors have learned to leave him alone; he never announces anything until he is certain of his results, and he can't work with a team. He says he thinks he has anti-gravity, and the company is galvanized. Other teams in other labs are working on the same project, but Max has it. His demonstration disk, about the size of a garbage-can lid, wobbles, lifts unevenly for a few inches, then settles, but that's enough. He has it, except for a few details. His estranged wife, who works for the same company, returns to him and talks about their future as wealthy celebrities after he wins the Nobel: he'll have his own research team to direct, the corner office. He'll be a global hero when everyone recognizes what it will mean to the world to have anti-gravity. When she left him, she said she couldn't stand having him mumbling to himself all the time and ignoring her. Now she is aglow. There is a symposium in Philadelphia which everyone attends, and where Max, always the outsider, stands alone, talking to himself much of the time. Following the symposium, security says a pair of scientists at B Company have changed direction; they are at Max's heels suddenly. Someone leaked enough to turn them around. Max is working longer and longer hours at the last few details; he is haggard and exhausted, and still alone in his own lab while others are checking his previous results. The pressure is on Max to finish first. Then someone calls him to come to the chief's office on the double, and there he finds the entire crew clustered around a television. The two researchers from B Company are beaming as a large disk floats around in the air. Max's wife cold-shoulders him on her way out, and others avoid looking at him. After a minute or two he slinks out, head bowed, shoulders slumped, defeated. In his own office, he picks up a model of his disk and puts it in his briefcase, then goes home. His house is empty. His wife has already cleared out her things. He closes blinds, locks the doors, puts the disk on the table, and sits on the sofa, gazing at it. He is thinking of the hotel in Philadelphia, where he stood at a mirrored planter and watched the reflections of the researchers from B Company draw near. When they were within range, he began to talk to himself. They froze, one clutching the other's arm. He watched them rush away. Now he takes out a handheld control and makes an adjustment. The disk on the table rises and floats lazily around the room. Max smiles.

This is a story of misdirection. It plays against the reader's expectations. Max has a problem, but it isn't the gizmo: it's the future he sees for himself when success is announced. He can't deprive the world of anti-gravity, however, so he finds a workable solution for his very personal problem. All he wants is to be left alone to do the work he loves. The reader was not lied to, just misled by his expectations about what people want.

There are many stories that seem to defy categories. Comic stories, satires, farces seemingly are contrary to everything I've said above, but on close examination and with thought, you'll find that the best ones almost always have an underlying serious issue and that they follow the same general guidelines as all other fiction.

But there is a real departure in the story that simply is irresistibly charming with no other redeeming virtues. Sometimes you can't explain such stories, explicate anything, find a theme, or analyze them. All we can do in their presence is bow and yield. And I certainly can't tell you how to write such a story.

Once Upon a Time

"Stop that," Tom growled, putting his book down. The wind and rain lashed trees into a frenzied dance. Sylvia hurried to finish coffee. The lights will go any minute. She didn't want to come. She wouldn't've come if she knew it was going to storm.

Not that she had a choice.

Miranda nipped his ankle again.

Moseley's poplar tree groaned and dropped a limb over the power line.

The lights disappeared.

That isn't the exact opening, but it's very close from what I recall and from the notes I made about it when it was workshopped. It is quite typical of many openings of stories that we critiqued. We generally tried to launch into our lectures using a story at hand to demonstrate points we wanted to make. We never had to wait longer than the first day for a story to provide more than enough material to discuss openings.

They are hard, and they are the only showcase most beginning writers get. The opening has to work because no matter how good the story might turn out to be, if no one reads beyond the first page, the story will not be published. Most often the showcase is no longer than the passage above.

We dissected those first pages mercilessly, word by word, line by line.

"'Stop that,' Tom growled." People don't growl words. Is Tom a talking dog? Boy? Old man? I don't know. Who is he talking to? I assume it is his story since he is the first one named.

"Wind and rain lashed…" Is he telling the wind to stop blowing? Are we out in a storm? Is he reading in a storm? Who sees the frenzied dance? There's a clue, though; enough light to see the dance.

"Sylvia hurried…" Who is she? Where are they? A tent? A cabin? Around a camp fire? In the same room? Is she drinking coffee or making it? Is Tom telling her to stop doing whatever she's doing with the coffee?

"The lights will go…" When? This is a declarative statement about the future. Who is thinking this? Why a tense change? Omniscient viewpoint?

"She didn't want to come…" When? She is already there.

"She wouldn't've come…" You might hear *would not have* like this, but many readers don't, and you should never write it that way. Also, the reader has to stop and puzzle it out. Spell it correctly.

And "if she knew" is wrong. When? Look up the use of past-perfect tense, and use it when appropriate. It should read, "She would not have come if she had known it was going to storm." "Not that she had a choice…" When? Choice about what? Coming? Doing whatever she's doing with coffee, although Tom told her to stop? Maybe she has a compulsion to fiddle with coffee and can't help herself? A sentence fragment that isn't self-explanatory is almost always a mistake. And a one-line paragraph is, too. There are four on this half-page.

"Miranda nipped…" We're back to Tom, apparently, or

is there another male around? This could be who he's telling to stop, but who is she? A two-year-old who likes to chew on his ankles? An animal?

"Moseley's poplar tree..." Are we back out in the storm? Are Moseley and Tom one and the same, or is this a new character? Where is the tree? The transitive verb *drop* means that something that was being held has been released and falls. People drop things, a cat may drop a mouse, but shelves don't drop books, tables don't drop glasses, and trees don't drop limbs.

"The lights disappeared." What lights? By the poplar tree? Distant lights can disappear; ambient light just goes off, and objects it illuminated disappear. And this seems to indicate that my assumption that it is still daylight was wrong, or else it doesn't matter if the lights go off.

There are four named characters, but we don't know yet whose story this is, what their relationship is to one another, anything about ages. We don't know anything about them except names. We don't know where they are, or if all four named people are present.

No one glancing through a stack of stories is going to analyze the openings, but if the sense of insecurity is strong because of many unanswered questions, awkward phrases, misused words, or many other reasons, if there is no compelling reason to turn the page, that story has had its chance, and the reader moves on to another one.

As it turned out the story that followed the above opening was pretty good. Miranda is an eighteen-year-old cat that Tom and Sylvia acquired as newlyweds, and one they both love. Their marriage is strained, and it could easily fall apart. They have gone to a mountain cabin to sort things out. During the storm, Tom accidentally steps on Miranda and she dies, and the marriage is over. It is Sylvia's story, more or less from her viewpoint, although the opening suggests that it will be omniscient viewpoint.

The writer said she had meant to say Sylvia was making coffee and she had left out a word by mistake. That makes no difference. The road to you-know-where is paved with good intentions, and no reader can intuit what you meant to say. The words on the page are all you have. She also said that she didn't come out and say Miranda was a cat until about page three or four on purpose, thinking it would be intriguing for the reader to wonder about it. That's wrong, too. The reader is looking for information, not a guessing game. The reader who had visualized a small child might feel angry to realize Miranda was a cat.

We cajoled, prodded, pleaded for better openings. I culled opening lines from well-known stories, Xeroxed them, passed them out, and we discussed what was accomplished in each one. I urge all beginning writers to do that, see what works for published stories. Sometimes the students argued back: Look at this by so and so, published, and it broke every rule. The answer is easy. So and so has earned the confidence of editors through a long period of writing good stories. She has mastered her craft and has enough technique at her fingertips to do whatever she wants to do and make it work. You, the beginning writer, have earned nothing yet. Your story is one of dozens or even hundreds of stories by other unknowns who have no brownie points, and you're all still in the slush pile, that heap of unsolicited stories the editor or a first reader will glance over in the hope that one might prove publishable. You will not be granted the same freedom at the beginning of your career that so and so has earned over the years. You have to start back there, playing by the rules until you prove yourself, exactly as she did.

The things the opening must do are really quite few. It must set the tone of the story. Ironic, elegiac, comic, adventurous—whatever tone the story demands should be established on the first page so that when the situation is being developed, the reader is not startled by finding a frenetic car chase in the middle of what had appeared to be a sad story about relationships. It should set a tone consistent with the meaning of the story. It must focus on one of the major story elements quickly: character, setting, or situation, or a combination of them. And it should establish a viewpoint that is maintained throughout. An accomplished writer will do much more than this, but these are basic. The opening has to start instantly to focus the attention toward the heart of the story. There is little neutral ground in the short story; every line, every word either helps or hurts it.

Countless times I wrote in the margin of the first page: *Set the stage.* We have to start off in a place where we can see the characters move about.

The list of what the opening should not do is endless. Our ingenious and perverse students kept coming up with new ways to frustrate a reader. (It was like the don't-put-beans-up-your-nose quandary. We didn't think we had to tell them *that.*) A few of the definitely don't-do-this things follow.

Don't have a meandering viewpoint, hopping like a flea from person to person. Even an omniscient viewpoint shifts for a definite reason when it moves from one to another. It is not random, and it is not accidental.

Don't confuse immediate setting with background and have your camera eye wander in, out, and about randomly. Don't leave the immediate setting to have a look at the distant landscape, drift back home, then leave again for no apparent reason.

Don't start with a lecture in anything—history, physics, biology—*anything.* Expository lumps anywhere are to be avoided if possible, but they are deadly in the opening.

Don't start in the middle of a scene, or in the middle of a conversation. That is why flashback openings are a mistake almost every time. You interrupt an ongoing scene to tell us something that happened earlier that results in the ongoing scene. Once started, the scenes should be concluded before you move on. An ongoing conversation is hard to catch up with. Who are these speakers, what is their relationship, what kind of voice should I be hearing in my head? Introduce them before they open their mouths.

Don't mislead the reader with false information or try to create suspense or arouse curiosity by withholding necessary information. What you arouse is distrust and annoyance.

Don't sprinkle a lot of neologisms around, made-up words that cannot be found in a dictionary. One woman said plaintively that one of her funny words was explained on page six, and another one in story three of the series she was writing. Who wants to read a story about a *quuza't'qu* without a clue about what it is until page six? And as for waiting for a different story, have mercy! A story must be self-contained. Many readers must have enough clues to visualize characters and the setting. Some need to be able to hear the words, to pronounce them, and if you throw unpronounceable syllables at them, they likely will move on to the next story.

Don't use words that only you and a few other people in your speciality can understand.

Don't use contractions if you can avoid them, and only sparingly no matter what. Never string together three words or more held by the glue of apostrophes. Readers have to stop and puzzle out what is missing. Once you invite a reader to step out of the story, that reader is not inclined to reenter it.

Don't have your character look into a mirror or other reflective surface in order to work in a description of her.

Don't let your character talk to an inanimate object or animal in order to give information to the reader about what is going on.

Don't play games with the sex of your character. If she is a female, don't get into a guessing game with the reader about it. As I mentioned earlier, some, possibly even most, readers visualize the characters, and if they think they are reading about a man and he stops to adjust his bra on page three, you probably will lose readers then and there. If your character truly is androgynous, even that won't hold for the entire story. Sooner or later a pronoun will have to be used if only to avoid the monotony of repeating the name constantly.

Enough. That's the tip of an iceberg that goes deep down into the ocean.

Damon used a red pen to mark manuscripts, but I used a pencil. There were several reasons. One was to make it apparent whose editing it was at a glance. Another was that if I changed my mind about something, I could erase my marks or comments. And I thought that red ink looked too much like mortal wounds. One night, reading for the next day, frustrated with bad openings, I drew a red line across the page.

The following day in class I explained I was playing the role of an editor with a magazine to put out who needed two or three stories to finish filling it. I started reading the slush pile and the red line marked where, as editor, I would stop reading a story and pick up the next one. That story would go back to the writer with a rejection slip eventually with no explanation. It is not in my job description to teach craft to a beginning writer, and I have neither the time nor the inclination to start now. So you, the writer of that story would never know how far I got, or what stopped me.

I continued saying, that, of course, as instructor, I would read the entire story as always, and that I would explain each and every time why I drew that line where I did. I got their attention. The students often compared their manuscripts to see where that line appeared, and those who had no red line let out a whoop of jubilation.

That line became known as The Red Line of Death. I used it every year after that. Damon began using it, too. It spoke more clearly than either of our voices had managed to do.

Beginning writers are not competing with the well-known established writers who can get away with whatever they choose. They compete among themselves. Your competition is with all the others in the slush pile, and if you can come up with a clear, straightforward opening that draws the reader in, you are already ahead of three out of four of your competitors.

Often that red line was followed by the words in the margin next to a paragraph farther along, sometimes pages deeper into the manuscript: *Start here.* Knowing where to start the story is as important as knowing how to start it. I usually say for a plotted story start soon before the precipitating event happens that sets the story in motion. Bring on your character, set a real stage that we can accept as plausible, and let us see how things are when they are they are stable before we see things in a chaotic situation. If my first glimpse of a character shows her hysterical and incoherent, I have no way of knowing if she has been driven to that stage. Since I don't know her, I can't know whether she is out of character, or if that is her normal behavior.

It does not take pages and pages to establish what normality is. A single mother and her son live in great poverty. She is at her wit's end with no food in the cottage and no money. She sends her son to market to sell the cow. We know enough at this point to imagine the rest of their situation and the setting. We don't need to know where the father is, or anything else about them. The boy meets the man with the magic bean, and a trade is made. That is the precipitating event, and now he can climb up the beanstalk.

Indiana Jones is teaching his university class when he is

summoned. That is enough. We know he is a professor and there is a real setting of his classroom. Now he can go off and have adventures.

We can see Dorothy, her aunt and uncle, the farmhands, the house. We have a character and a real setting. Now the tornado can blow her away.

In the case of the unplotted story, the writer must know the significance of what is to be shown, and care taken of what events or days will reveal that significance. The writer must know what to leave out as well as what to include.

In my story, "Ladies and Gentlemen, This Is Your Crisis," I open with a woman entering her house with groceries for the weekend. She turns on a wall television screen on her way to the kitchen where she turns on a small television, which she watches as she puts the groceries away—frozen TV dinners, sandwich meats, bread and beer. She is catching up to the action of four people who are in a wilderness area, competing to see who will get out first and win the prize.

(An aside here: I didn't steal anyone's idea. My story is more than twenty years old.)

What I wanted to do in the opening was establish a middle-aged woman who has a dead-end factory job, and the setting that the story demands. I left out details of her work, how she moves about the city, everything except the place where she lives, and the weekend provisions she has bought, because everything else was irrelevant to the story I was telling.

This story is one of the variety of a-day-in-the-life-of stories. In my story, it is a weekend in the life of a couple, and next weekend will be about like this one, and the next and the next...

You have to know what is relevant to what you intend to reveal about the characters and the situation you are telling us about, and leave out anything that isn't relevant. It could be that you will show only a few hours, or perhaps months, but the principle is the same.

Also the first few lines must be as controlled and informative as those about an adventure story to come.

Whatever kind of story you are writing, you have to provide information from the opening line onward, and the sooner you set the stage, the freer you are to move about in it, and the more likely we are to suspend disbelief and follow along.

Body Count

It surprised me how often the observed story was written by students. By that I mean a story in which the narrator is not the protagonist, not the one the story is about, but merely an observer of events. A story is by its nature distant. The writer conceives of it through a process that is largely unconscious; there must be a very conscious effort to translate images, impulses, emotions to words in a meaningful way. It is a mediated activity that requires a certain level of education and intelligence. The reader in turn must go through the same process in reverse, translate marks on paper to images, emotions, impulses, and meaning, another mediated activity that ensures that the story is already one step removed, distant. A movie, by comparison, is immediate, the impact immediate for literate or illiterate people alike.

To remove the story yet another step by telling it through an observer instead of the one directly affected will distance it further, and is seldom successful. It was a method often used in the nineteenth century, but it has fallen out of favor.

If the narrator has no part to play, nothing at stake, nothing to gain or lose in the story, why have him or her there?

Yet we frequently saw such stories at Clarion. Often the narrator acted as a news reader, and the events being told were of a cataclysmic nature, but no matter how devastating the events, these stories fell flat. We want to read about people who can influence events, or be influenced by them directly. It is hard to get impassioned through reading a history of the French revolution, but in the hands of a master storyteller like Dickens, who puts characters on the scene and lets us feel their anguish and fear, it comes alive.

Stories told by a detached observer can rarely arouse suspense or create tension in the reader who wants the vicarious experience of someone living through the events.

A student wrote a story about a Mars expeditionary crew returning to Earth after a successful mission. There is a malfunction of equipment, and their oxygen will run out in a few days, while the remaining trip will take ten days. It is a real problem, with competently drawn characters and the situation presented with care. Yet the story failed. By page four, the situation was clear, and the decision was made to sedate everyone not necessary to maintain the flight, lower the temperature for them, and reduce their oxygen consumption. I have no idea if the solution would really work, but for story purposes it was well enough thought out and explained to appear plausible, and the solution was carried out on page four or five of a fifteen-page story.

Basically the story ended there. The two wakeful crew members spent the rest of the trip checking gauges and doing other routine chores. The story started with a suspenseful situation, and still failed.

Plotted stories all have certain things in common regardless of the subject matter. They all involve conflict. Man against nature, man against culture, man against himself, man against other men, and so on. In the above story, it was man against technology or environment. Good plotted stories involve conflict, and they also have a growing sense of tension created by real suspense, or at least a mounting uneasiness until there is a climax and relief. That is where the above story failed. The suspense ended as soon as the crew members were sedated. The next ten pages were anticlimactic.

There are many ways to create suspense, and the most commonly used one may be to raise the stakes. A small problem evolves into a much bigger one as the story develops.

For instance, a man borrows a few dollars from the till at work, with every intention of repaying it on Monday when he returns to his job. Over the weekend, an audit reveals that thousands of dollars are missing, and our man is caught in a dilemma that becomes a crisis. He can't return the ten dollars, because investigators have been called in. He can't confess to borrowing ten dollars, for fear of being accused of stealing the larger amount. He does not dare take a lie detector test, because he has a guilty conscience. The stakes have been raised.

Piling on more of the same menace creates suspense. In the Hitchcock movie *The Birds*, first there is one bird behaving erratically. It attacks a woman. Then several birds attack people, and finally there are immense flocks of birds attacking. Horror films and horror stories often use this method. Sometimes the effect is more ludicrous than frightening: a little blood, then more blood, and finally oceans of blood.

Another method of increasing tension or suspense is through simple escalation. Two brothers have sharp words; then one pushes the other. One tears up the other's room, they have a real fight, and finally one of them is oiling a gun. It has a sense of inevitability about it even as the tension rises.

Racing against time always creates suspense. Someone has to defuse the bomb in the next two minutes. Or someone has to get to the hospital before he bleeds to death. Get the sheep in before the blizzard hits. Clear the valley before the dam breaks. Stop the wedding before the ceremony is finalized. Whatever the situation is, the ticking clock adds suspense.

Another way is by increasing apprehension about what is to come. Big Bad Bart with his gang of brutal outlaws is heading toward town, and the townspeople start preparing, telling stories of Bart's various exploits in other places. They hide their nubile young daughters, bury the silverware, board up the windows, load their guns, and all the while Bart is getting closer. It might be Hells Angels on the way, aliens, or any other person or group seen as the enemy. It could be a plague, or a swarm of locusts, anything drawing closer that characters fear to the point of panic.

It may be that the danger of the situation does not change, as in the case of a serial killer who always claims the same kind of victim and commits the same kind of gruesome murder. The rising suspense is caused by the failure of the investigators to stop him over and over, with each new attempt a little more desperate than the last. If a sympathetic character is the next obvious target, the suspense rises higher.

In any event, whatever the subject matter, there is a growing suspense, a rising tension until the climax. Without it, the story will be seen as static, and it will fail.

There are as many ways to kill suspense as there are to create it. One certain way is through a plot loop.

A woman wrote a story about a husband-and-wife team of researchers who had made a momentous discovery, and were in the middle of an intense struggle about whether to release it. Ethical problems were apparent, and they were in a bind. Then the man goes off to a family gathering, and for three or four pages he is surrounded by a whole new set of characters who have nothing to do with the story. He returns and picks up the struggle where it left off. That is a typical plot loop. And it is deadly for a story.

We often saw plot loops, and they could always be snipped

right out and never missed. The writer confessed that she had not known how to indicate that by Monday they had not yet resolved their problem. Also, the story would have been no more than three or four pages if she had resolved the problem too soon. The answer? Use a line break to indicate the passage of time or to indicate that we are now in a different place, or any other discontinuity. Or simply say something like, "By Monday, they knew they had to decide."

What you don't do is introduce extraneous material to account for the passage of time. And if the story is then too short or too simple, perhaps you have not developed the characters fully, or explored all the options or the complications that each option would present.

There are conventions in any art form, those things we accept without question. The overage, overweight soprano playing the role of a young beautiful heroine in opera; the fact that in movies, the stars seldom have pasts or families—they come on full grown, and the action proceeds; in Old West movies, the cowboy hero has an endless supply of bullets. And so on. These are conventions. In short fiction, there are conventions also.

One is that the first named character is the one the story is about. If John is introduced and has a paragraph or two, we have every expectation that it is his story. If Mary then comes along and the focus shifts to her, we feel disoriented and have to make a mental adjustment. Or, as was often the case, the story goes along about John, and at the end a different character takes the stage to explain things, or to solve the problem, or become a significant player in some other way. We are left wondering what happened to John and his problematic situation.

Deus ex machina is a useful phrase to remember. It never works to have a new character solve the hero's problem, or have fate step in, or a miracle, or God. If it is John's problem, let him deal with it if he can or fail if that is what the story demands.

Students often thought that killing off characters added great suspense to their stories, and we had to tell them repeatedly that it was not so. At one Clarion, I counted twenty-eight dead bodies in the first few stories turned in, and we had to say firmly, no more killing. Sometimes they did not know what else to do with characters, so they killed them in a variety of ways. Deaths by drowning, by car accidents, airplane crashes, storms, gunfire, poison.... Strangely, none of the stories were mysteries, just folks going around knocking each other off.

Or they killed off one character in order to teach another a bitter lesson. A young man's careless act leads to the death of his best friend, and he learns not to be so careless. Or he learns that driving and drinking don't mix, or something else. You cannot treat death that cavalierly in fiction, unless it is a farce, or a puzzle where no one cares anyway about the newly departed. Anything as riveting and important as a death cannot be trivialized as background material for a story.

The threat of the paper tiger is always a big mistake. A husband and wife have become frightened watching television news about a series of burglaries where people were brutalized. A car pulls into the driveway without lights, no motor noise, and they assume the worst. They turn off lights in an effort to make the house appear empty. She searches frantically for the phone while he loads his gun, and the suspense mounts. Then their teenage son yells that he is home, and why are the lights all turned off? He ran out of gas and coasted into the driveway. Paper tiger. And the reader has expended a lot of energy and wasted adrenaline, getting anxious about what was going to happen next. That reader feels cheated every time. Don't cry wolf unless a wolf is at the gate.

The threat has to be real, and it has to put the character in jeopardy. It can be the loss of a job, the dissolution of a marriage, a failed space mission, death, loss of honor and self-respect, but whatever the menace, it has to be real for the character, and it has to be meaningful. The situation cannot build toward a climax and then pop like a soap bubble.

The character has to be qualified to do whatever is required in the story. We don't want to read about Superman rescuing a cat from a tree, and we don't want to read about a child who has to save the universe from aliens. Give them tasks worthy of their abilities, or abilities they develop by necessity that they might not have shown before, like a timid person who becomes heroic when a loved one is threatened.

We have to know what the limits are. The invisible man leaves footprints in the snow. In a story of magic, there have to be limits, also. When is it effective, and when is it not? If everything is possible to the magician, nothing is interesting. There has to be vulnerability of some kind. The richest man in the world cannot buy the love of the one woman he yearns for, or the respect of his father, or something. The most beautiful woman is fearful of the first sign of aging. The strongest man could be rendered helpless against a small child pointing a finger of accusation at him. There are always limits that can be used to help create suspense, and if unexamined or ignored, they can destroy it.

One story had a woman who went to the airport to have lunch with her father who had a two- or three-hour layover. She is seen by her husband's coworker, who mentions seeing her with a strange man to the husband. He leaps to a terribly wrong conclusion and has a one-night stand with an old girlfriend. If either of these people had said the obvious thing to each other in the beginning, there would not have been a story. We often saw stories like that. One question, or one comment early, no story, and normal people do mention things like, "Oh, by the way, Dad is passing through tomorrow." Or ask things like, "What were you doing at the airport?"

The story we saw turned very violent and mean, and it did not work. It might have worked if we had seen the couple becoming estranged and suspicious to the point of insane behavior, but as written, the cause and effect were disproportionate. A misunderstanding led to the death of a character. Crime and punishment should be commensurate, or the character is perceived as too neurotic, or even too psychotic, to create suspense.

It doesn't have to be an overt threat or menace that creates suspense. Sometimes a deserving character trying to achieve a goal desperately wanted or needed is enough. Virtue may be its own reward in life, but in stories we want to see a more tangible reward. He wants desperately to make the team, or she wants to get into premed school. When we see a sympathetic character struggling against great odds, we want that character to succeed. We want the mission to Mars to be a success; we want to see the experiment work, the weakling subdue the bully, the humble poor man bring down the arrogant wealthy one, the boy and girl get together in the end and live happily ever after.

But it can't be an easy victory. The obstacles must be difficult, and the protagonist must win through his or her own efforts.

Beginning writers often confuse predictability with inevitability. A plot-driven story relies on the predictable almost every time, with violence or at least confrontations as regular as waves tumbling to shore. There has been a lull; the Pretty Young Thing, usually scantily clad, is alone in the house; it's time to bring in the psychopathic killer. Or the hero is making his escape; it's time to have three cars in hot pursuit for another car chase. Or it's time to set off the fireworks, bombs, explosions. Or time for someone to go down into the dark cellar to see what's making that noise. The plot determines the actions, the characters are little more than game pieces being moved about.

At the height of our killing spree, one of the students wrote a satire that summarized the problem. Three heroic space explorers who have been together for a long time are joined by a newcomer on a dangerous mission. It was predictable from his first appearance that the untried new member was born to die young. And he did.

These stories get published now and then, and they are what people mean when they categorize science fiction as a subliterary genre directed at adolescent males. Action and violence do not generate real suspense when they are contrived for effect.

In the story of inevitability, the characters determine the actions. They often act against their will, against their better judgment, but they are compelled to act by their own inner needs. A woman has finally attained a coveted position in a research lab after years of struggling. She learns that her boss, the Great Man, has falsified test results. Knowing she is putting herself at risk, she collects the data she needs to prove her case, but then she realizes that she is also endangering her two children. There can be a growing menace, subtle threats, not-so-subtle incidents that all add to the suspense, but finally, however she decides to move will be determined by how she was developed throughout the story. If her love for her children is the factor that influences her to burn the evidence, we should feel that it was inevitable based on what we had already learned about her. If she proceeds to become a whistle-blower, that, too, should appear absolutely inevitable. The character determines the outcome in either event. In this kind of story the conflict is real and deep, and the suspense is just as real.

Unplotted stories have a rising tension also, but this time in the reader, not the characters in the story. Sometimes you want to step in and shake a character and say, "Stop this! Don't you see what you are doing to yourself?" As you get more and more involved with the characters, you often can see clearly where their actions are leading, but there is no way you can intervene, and you simply hope that one or the other character will grasp what you see or understand.

Or you get interested, thinking the character is benign perhaps, only to realize that actions you thought were kindly meant were really manipulative, and you have to rethink your own interpretation of human behavior.

Whatever the substance of the unplotted story is, the writer must involve the reader, make the reader want to see what, if anything, is going to happen next, if the character will escape the futile life he is living and do something else, or if she will come to realize that there is no way to pacify an insanely jealous, overcontrolling man.

When the reader is groping for understanding or searching for meaning in the lives of the characters, and the moment of truth of the story arrives, that reader has a reaction as satisfying as the climax of a suspense story brings, even if that satisfaction is expressed by nothing more than a nod, a quiet, "Ah, I see." Solving a riddle in the great mysterious tangle of human life can be especially satisfying. Now the reader can leave the characters to their own devices, step back, and relax with a new understanding.

When you have become interested, involved, and there is no moment of truth, it is as if your friend started to tell you about an event that was important, and was called away before she could finish the tale. You feel frustrated, perhaps even angry that your emotions were aroused with no relief offered. That moment of truth may come during the reading, or it may be delayed until after the last word, but it brings an emotional reprieve when it does arrive. That is the climax of the unplotted story, and it is as necessary as the climax of the most suspenseful ones, and like those other climaxes, it has to be approached step by careful step so that it appears inevitable, and also surprising.

Please Speak Up

A student wrote a story in which a teenaged boy is walking along a riverbank at dusk, with a deep dark forest close on the other side of him. The boy is terrified, and the story was infused with a sense of terror and dread as darkness continued to fall and the river became a black surface. The student then put crocodiles in the water, and had the boy in the story direct his fear at them. The story instantly lost its power. The fear of the unknown, of what lay within the impenetrable forest, what lurked beneath the opaque surface of the water was much more powerful than the fear of crocodiles.

The other students picked the story apart as the critique went around the circle. Why was the boy there? He was obviously mid-American, and the forest and river were out of Michigan or somewhere else in temperate mid-America, hardly a setting for a crocodile-infested river. Why was he walking in the forest when it was getting dark? Where was he going? What was in the forest? On and on. Such palpable frustration was more than just the sense of failure of the story, but almost as if the others in the class had felt on the verge of a wonderful truth, and then were given a trivial and implausible fib.

The boy was not running, obviously not in flight from an ax-wielding maniac. He had not picked up a tree branch to ward off a cougar or mad dog, or anything else that could be fought. The students had not raised these points, but they had sensed that the menace was not a mundane or material threat.

The writer had no answers for any of the questions. He knew only that the terror-filled scene had come to him, and he had added the crocodiles to try to account for the fear in his attempt to turn the surreal into a story.

Later, in conference with us, he explained that he often had fragments of stories like that, and he had been afraid to do anything with them except try to add an explanation for the fear, the joy, or whatever powerful emotion always seemed to be part of them. To tamper with them in any way, he feared, would take away whatever power they held.

I don't live by the clock. I work late hours at night and get up when I wake without much regard for what time it is. On those occasions when I have to get up early and set the alarm at bedtime, I invariably wake before it goes off. I know many others who say the same thing happens with them. It is as if something in us is keeping track of the time while we sleep.

Most of us have had the experience of seeing a familiar person approach, only to find to our dismay that her name has slipped out of memory. Embarrassing, but common. We cover ourselves as best we can and move on, then have the name pop up an hour later, or the next morning, or perhaps just minutes later.

Or you sniff anise and find yourself deluged by memories from childhood of Christmas cookies baking, something you have not thought of in years perhaps.

Say you have a real problem that you have been mulling over for a long time and still cannot solve. We all know the saying—sleep on it, so you finally put it out of mind and go to bed, and in the morning, you have your answer. Many scientific discoveries have been made in such a way. First you give it your full attention, immerse yourself in it, then put it aside, and the answer comes to you.

We are going to skip the entire, ever-controversial, never-ending argument over mind–body, conscious–unconscious, rationalism–Jungian psychology, right brain–left brain distinctions, and all other theoretical and philosophical explanations. We will also skip physiology, synapses formation, neural pathways, and such and talk about direct experience.

For the sake of this section, when I refer to you, I mean that thinking, verbal person who writes and talks and is reading this passage. I don't mean that other part of your psyche whose form of communication is through images, dreams, impulses, impressions without form, that other part that remains wordless and may, furthermore, fail to recognize your words. For the sake of this section, I'll consider it as another being, separate from you, even if forever united with you. Damon referred to that other part as Fred, but I don't think there is a Fred living in my brain. I think of it as my silent partner, or SP.

SP is like an overworked file clerk scurrying around in your psyche taking care of things, feeding you the right file on call, nudging you to remember an appointment, filling in the blanks of your memory—sometimes belatedly, but more often faithfully—giving you dreams about every ninety minutes throughout sleep, furnishing your daydreams with images, and so on.

You want to arrive at a good working relationship with that silent partner. For one thing, SP has complete access to your entire database that is made up of everything you have experienced in your whole life, and you will need SP's help more often than you realize. For another, you cannot produce art without it. You could fill in the blanks of a complete outline and have what might look like a story, but it would have the same relationship to literary art as painting-by-numbers does to visual art. The finished work might show skill in following an outline, flawless grammar, good deliberately chosen words, but it would be mechanical and empty. And finally, you must cultivate SP because it is a wonderful problem solver and collaborator.

Although SP has found ways to communicate with you, you can never be certain you can communicate to SP. It does not use language or words to communicate with you, and from all indications, it does not comprehend words you direct at it or, at least, it does not respond in a meaningful way to your direct orders or pleas expressed in words. It is aware of you and everything you do instant by instant, but you are never aware of it directly, only of the effects it has on you. Even if it seems that two-way communication is impossible, with reflection it becomes obvious that it does grasp yes or no, acceptance or rejection.

Start with habituation. Say you have made the decision to put aside two hours three days a week and declare that time yours, your time to write. You go wherever you can write and work at it. If you are not actively writing a story, rewrite an old one, or analyze something you did in the past or someone else's work to see how that person did it. Dedicate that time to writing and nothing else, and keep doing it on schedule. If you are faithful to your own timetable, the day will come when, if you yield to the temptation to watch a show on television or play cards, or do something else, you may begin to feel uncomfortable, your mind may wander, or you may become restless. SP is signaling that this is your writing time. If you yield often and ignore the signals, SP stops reminding you. If you recognize the signal and go back to work, SP will remind you a little more forcefully the next time you yield. Recognizing the signal does not mean you are aware of it necessarily. What you may be aware of is that you are uncomfortable, and when you go to work, your discomfort is eased, but that is enough. Accepted signals get stronger; ignored signals fade out.

You have nothing to worry about if you get no such signals while on vacation, traveling, having in-laws visit, or any of the other events that interrupt your daily routine. It appears that SP grants time off for such events in your life, and the signals either are not sent, or are too feeble to register. When the routine is reentered later, they return.

Probably all your life you have imagined snippets of stories, possible scenes, situations, glimpses of characters, story ideas, images and have done little or nothing with them. Most writers have very active daydreams for years before they actually begin to write. When you begin to accept the ideas, snippets and all, and work or play with them, manipulate them, more will follow and they will become stronger and more compelling. Your silent partner's offering has been accepted. You have communicated through acceptance. It is as if your acceptance has empowered it, and the next time it will be more forceful.

Your silent partner is amoral—it has no real esthetic sense, no chronological sense, no relative worth sense; a pebble is as good as a pearl to it. Also it does not know anything you have not taught it through your life experiences. If you read widely in a variety of subjects, it has a wealth of materials to offer back to you, often in strange and wonderful new combinations that you might never have considered. If your reading consists of only one or two favorite writers, it has that as its source material. If you read little or nothing, just watch television, for example, that content makes up much of its database. If it offers trivia and you accept and write that, it will offer more of the same invariably.

This is where the partnership comes in. You have to examine the ideas that seemingly come from out of nowhere, that are actually from your silent partner, and say yes or no to them.

This requires the rational, verbal, conscious you. You can't tell SP directly what you want; you can demonstrate what you don't want by your rejection, or signify what you find exciting, or perhaps simply worthwhile, by your acceptance. You are not born with the skill to know which ideas are worthy of writing, which are too trivial to bother with; that judgment takes time and patience as your own critical faculties are honed and developed, but you will find that as you become more demanding of yourself, the material you receive from SP—impulses, ideas, images, sequences, whatever form it takes—will become more complex and interesting.

Probably you will also find that one day when you have been working, writing well, feeling good about it, if you are interrupted, or when it is time to stop, you will feel that you have been gone. You have been somewhere else, in some kind of alternative head space, that someone else has been filling in for you. Perhaps your sense of time has been distorted; it is hard to believe that three hours have passed. Or perhaps the headache you had earlier was forgotten, then returns when you leave your work. Or a nagging worry was put aside and now surges back.

I have often said that I, this person who does the shopping and gardening and attends to the daily chores that arise, I am not the one who writes my stories. That is my writing persona, the person I become when I am writing. She is much smarter than I am, and she has a memory I wish I had available all the time. She can use words I cannot even pronounce. She seems oblivious of minor aches and pains, and she is disdainful of the clock.

Every year at Clarion the visiting instructors give a reading, sometimes to the public, sometimes just for the students. One year the story I read was about a young woman who has never reconciled with her own childhood of humiliation and pain caused by a brutal father. Now, in love with a man who wants to marry her, she can't make up her mind. At a family celebration, she confronts her father and her brother, who was beaten into submission and is now doing the same thing to his child. The father is a man of wealth and influence, a lawyer, and her brother is following in his footsteps. They are people of substance, highly regarded in the community. She dreams that she is in a silent walled garden trying desperately to reach doors that are closing. She fails to get to them before they close all the way, and she is imprisoned in an eerily silent garden with no escape. When she wakes from her dream, she flees her father's house, drives aimlessly, and finally stops at a motel, where she at last reaches for the phone to call the child services agency to report her brother. The story ended there.

The title of the story was "The Great Doors of Silence," published in *Redbook* magazine. Glenn Wright was the director that year, and he asked the class if her call would save the child. There was no clear answer because I had not given one in the story. Then Glenn said, "Well, of course not. Her name is Cass. She's Cassandra crying in the wilderness."

I had not known that. The name had come to me, and I had used it without another thought, but my writing persona had known and made use of it. More recently I named a character Erica, and in the course of the novel she acquired the nickname of Rikki, and again my writing persona had helped. Her name "just came" to me. Rikki Tikki Tavi of Rudyard Kipling fame was fearless and deadly protecting his own.

I have a pretty good working relationship with my own silent partner. I like being in that alternative state of awareness when my writing persona takes over. I think that in that state, the gap between you and your silent partner closes, if not altogether, then much of the way. It is exhilarating to use your whole brain, or even simply most of it.

But you have to work with it, work on it, and the first step may be habituation, your recognition of signals and signs and your acceptance or rejection of them, then your acceptance or rejection of images, snatches of memory, even sequences that are dreamlike and surreal. They may be very beautiful or they may be frightening, but they are not stories as given.

Your silent partner cannot write stories. It is nonverbal and nonrational. It cannot organize the wealth of dream material and memories at its disposal into a series of happenings that make sense. In a sleeping dream or even in a waking daydream, you may be euphoric one moment with the sensation of floating, flying, deliriously happy, and in the next moment plunging to earth in terror. Both apparently are universal dreams. Both are loaded with emotion and power, but they do not make a story. Your very rational mind has to manipulate them, find cause and effect, find a character who can express that joy or fear in a plausible way.

Often beginning writers recognize the power of this material and are afraid to change it, to manipulate it in any way, and instead try to translate it directly from dream imagery to waking actions. It will rarely work as a direct translation.

I urged students to treat this rich material the same way they would treat the results of research. Use what you need of it, change what you must change, and don't treat it as untouchable. It is a gift from you to you, and it is the nature of gifts that once proffered and accepted, they become the property of the receiver to do with as she pleases.

The writer of the crocodile story knew only that it was a sequence that had come to him, and he had added the crocodiles in an attempt to account for the fear and to try to turn the surreal directly into story. He had been afraid to manipulate the material and use it in a meaningful way. To do that, he would have had to question what emotional or psychological truth the boy was trying to deny or escape from. The other students were especially hard on the story because they had recognized the significance of the fear and dread, and they were very disappointed that instead of revealing what it meant, the story had been reduced to something trivial and without meaning.

Your silent partner can give you vivid, powerful, nonverbal material, but it cannot tell you what to do with it, how to use it in stories. It cannot tell you what the sequences and images mean. That takes a conscious, rational mind; it takes technique and control deliberately applied. You may find that some of the images and fragments are frightening when you examine them closely and accept the meaning you derive from them. Things you would never admit to, desires you have to deny, fears you can't express, but that's what lies at the heart of good fiction. Your readers have the same problems expressing those things, and through fiction they are afforded the opportunity to experience them indirectly and maintain personal safety. This can be cathartic for writer and reader alike.

To become a successful writer, you must cultivate the partnership between that nonverbal wealth of emotional material, and your own consciously applied control of it—and the sooner, the better. Without it, your stories will be flat and mechanical, and quite likely they will be trivial and unpublished. With it, when you begin to examine this material and express it through your characters in meaningful ways, your stories will become richer, with much greater depth, and possibly approach the universality that writers strive for.

We always liked to ask the students how they wrote, what methods they used, and as they went around the circle, most of the answers were already familiar to everyone: start with an idea, or with a phrase, or an outline, and so on. Invariably there would be someone, often more than one, who said she didn't know. No real method came to mind. She had pictures in her mind and told stories about them, and sometimes they worked as fiction; more often they didn't.

When it came to my turn, I said that was how I wrote everything. Images form, and if they have emotionally compelling power, I seize them, knowing they mean I have a story working. At that point, I never know if I will be writing a novel or a short story, or something in between. That always comes much later.

All through school, we had to write papers starting with a simple theme or thesis. On its approval, we turned in an outline, and from there went to a draft, and finally a finished draft. I tried many times, but I simply could not do it that way. Instead, I wrote the article or story, outlined what I had written, and then found the theme. I handed them in in the proper order, and I never confessed that I had done it backward. Now, after many years of practice, I no longer have to write the entire thing first; I can think it through until I know it thoroughly, and at that point I can outline it if there is any reason to do so.

Working from images, to scenes, to incidents, then situation and finally plot is the only way I can write anything. And plot, the chronological story line, for me always comes last.

One young woman said she thought of it as working with snapshots from a story not yet written. I think that is a fine way to describe it. But it does take some thought. And I have found that it takes patience. Images cannot be forced.

For those who want to try this, I can give a few pointers, and since I have already given a bare-bones synopsis of the failed story above, I'll use that to illustrate my points.

First, try to isolate the emotional response that is often attached to the image. The writer of the crocodile story knew what that was: terror. Sometimes it is a little harder to identify an emotion.

The next step is to stop the motion if there is any and examine the person and the immediate surroundings from wherever your view of the scene is. In the scene as written, the boy was average in every way, dark hair, T-shirt, jeans, Reeboks, not carrying anything, no backpack. He was shown face on, coming toward the point of view, his expression a study in fear, with his gaze darting this way and that.

I always ask myself who sees this. If there is no one there to observe, I usually assume that the character I am seeing is the protagonist. Sometimes there is another person through whose eyes I am seeing the scene or image, and that person is the protagonist. In the story about the boy in the woods, he is alone and is the protagonist.

Now, look around the boy, first at the riverside, without shifting the point of view. What can you tell about the river? Swift and clear? Sluggish and brown? Wide as a major river, narrow? If this is an image in your own mind, answers to the questions will begin to form as you pose the questions. The river might be thirty feet across, with muddy banks indicating low water; rocks might cause ripples, and so on. Then look at the opposite bank to see what is over there. More woods? A field? Another path like the one the boy is on? You keep questioning the entire scene to see how many answers are forthcoming. Do the same thing with the forest on the other side of the boy. What kind of forest? Deciduous trees? What kind of under story? Ferns, brambles? Rocks? The boy is in a T-shirt, no jacket, presumably it is warm weather, summer, so the forest should be in full leaf.

When you can get nothing more from the immediate scene, look behind the boy into the distance as far as your vision permits and question it, then when there is nothing more, turn around and look in the direction the boy is going and do it again. The whole point is that you have been given an emotionally compelling image, and you have to play detective and wrest from it every detail it can yield. You don't know what any of it means yet, or where it will fit into a story, but you can't force meaning on it, or introduce a consciously arrived-at menace.

In this scenario, with an average boy about sixteen years old, you have to start thinking about what would induce such terror. You don't provide the answer; you ask the question. And if a facile answer pops up—crocodiles—you have to reject it and demand something more in keeping with what you know about woods like those woods, and boys like that boy.

You should question where the boy has come from and where he is going. Is anyone waiting for him? Where is the river, the woods? What state? How far from the city? And so on. Whatever you can think of to question. Don't try to supply answers; just raise the questions.

You have to be patient and wait for the next tidbit to come to you, but if you persist with the opening image and keep thinking about it, questioning it, the next bit will more than likely arrive with the same clarity that the first one had. When that happens, you will recognize it as another piece of the puzzle you are working on. It could be a totally different location, with other people involved, but it will have its own emotional impact, and you treat it the same way you did the first image and question every aspect of it thoroughly.

It may take several days to get all the pieces you need in order to start weaving a web of a story line around them, or it could happen quickly. In any event, you can't force the material with conscious meaning until you are certain nothing more is forthcoming, and then your rational, deliberating mind has its own task, to travel from one scene to another to make up the story. It is as if that silent partner, your collaborator, is telling you that it's your turn to do something with these images it has provided.

How do you recall a movie? Usually by first remembering a snapshot, a vivid scene. Like Thelma and Louise sailing out over the cliff in the Thunderbird. Then you back up and recall the landscape filled with police cars closing in on them, and then on to another scene until finally you have all the pieces and you can rearrange them in chronological order. That is exactly the way this method of storytelling works, except that you don't consciously know the story yet, and you have to create it from the snapshots your brain serves up.

The snapshots or images probably won't be in any sensible order—that is your task when you have gathered them all in—and you may find that the snapshot that came to mind first fits at the end of the story, or in the midsection, not the beginning.

It is as the sculptor said: You remove everything that isn't David. In the case of the work of fiction, you discover everything that belongs in the story, and then you piece it together to make it coherent, as if the story is truly already written, and you're in the process of recalling it to consciousness and restoring the words.

Not many students could grasp this method, but for those who did, it was a tremendous relief to find that it was okay to work this way. One woman was nearly in tears when she thanked me. She had been on the verge of giving up, certain that she could not become a writer, because she could not use any of the methods she had read about or heard discussed. She had not learned to wait for more than one striking image, and always rushed into a story too soon, which was what the writer had done with the crocodile story. Their stories had not worked yet, although they had remarkable imagery.

At some point, you will probably find that you are returning to one or another of the earlier images and fleshing it out with information you have gained from subsequent pictures in your head. That is okay, too. Once you start consciously manipulating the material, you may have to change parts of it to fit the story you are telling. But it is yours to work with. It is not sacrosanct, untouchable. It is raw material to be used.

I'll go to a real novel I wrote. The opening image that led to the novel *Where Late the Sweet Birds Sang* was of three women talking, and the feeling that came with it was one of hopelessness and longing. The women were obviously three generations of a family, a young woman of about twenty, her mother, and her grandmother with a striking resemblance one to another. The setting was a sprawling farmhouse, and the observer I discovered was David, the protagonist of the first section of the novel. Eventually I had to find out why he felt longing and hopelessness. If he loved the young woman, why didn't he act on his love? As I probed and other images came to mind, I saw them tumbling in a real fight. I saw them standing under a great white oak tree, and eventually I came to realize that they were cousins, and in that family cousins were forbidden to marry. Another vivid image was of three girls who looked like the first one, but these three were identical. I had no idea yet what the novel was going to be, where I was going with it, but I knew I was working on a novel. I had been reading a lot about the DNA research going on, the Watson and Crick book, *The Double Helix*, and I had been reading about kibbutzim in Israel and the children who were growing up in them. My brain began serving up ideas from those sources to complement the pictures that were still forming.

When I began to tell myself the whole story, some of the images belonged in the first part, others close to the end, or somewhere in the middle, and it was my job to sort them out, to change what I had to change to make them fit, and to weave them all together in a coherent story. I liken this part to working a jigsaw puzzle. You have all the pieces spread out and have to discover the borders first, the boundaries of the story, and then find where the pieces fit within them.

Both Damon and I always said that however a writer goes about it, whatever method is effective is the proper method for that writer. It doesn't have to conform to a preconceived idea about how one should write. I rarely start a novel on page one of the first chapter. My sections are numbered from *one* to wherever I stop. Eventually I put them in order. But I have no need to write them the way readers read them, starting at the beginning, going to the end, stopping.

I have to get a sentence right, not necessarily the first sentence, just a sentence that might fit in anywhere. I have to have the tone, the voice, and then I can write. Sometimes I've had the story in my head for days before I have that one sentence that lets me go on.

If you find the opening is too difficult, it just won't do what you want it to do, start somewhere else that is more interesting to you, and get back to the opening later. If you can't write a section, skip it, write a different one. The material, the story, characters, plot, images, snapshots—all of it is yours to handle the best way you can, any way that suits you and works for you. You can rearrange pieces as long as it takes to make it a complete story. Renumber them as often as necessary until you know exactly where each piece fits. No one has to know, or ever should guess when they read a finished story, what a mess it was in the creation.

Keep in mind that the wonderful, powerful image that first came to you may be the high point of a story, and the story should build to it, not start with it. And if your brain is feeding you strange and mysterious pictures, accept them and work with them. Consider them target points, and you have to create the bridges that will lead from one to another. You may end up with an original story that never could have happened with the fill-in-the-blanks outline method. That is a great partnership to nourish, your rational mind and your own surreal nonverbal mind.

What does not work is to believe that if those snapshots or images come in a series that at first glance appears to be coherent, you accept that sequence as a story. It isn't yet. It's a sequence, a series of surreal, tenuously linked images that on examination most often prove to be as irrational as dreams. They are dreams, waking dreams. You probably have noticed that when you start to relate a dream to someone else, that person's eyes start to glaze, and an absent expression crosses his face. No one else feels the same impact from dreams that they have had on the dreamer. The symbolism and images are extremely private, and without deliberate conscious effort, they fail to speak to anyone else. It is your job as a writer to recast those dream images so that they carry the same power to the reader that they had on you.

One part of the mind can furnish the symbolism, images, snapshots, but it takes a rational, thinking, verbal mind to form them into a story that will be coherent and meaningful.

Beyond the Five W's

I think of those classes often, but never any specific year. It's one big, ever-expanding Clarion family of hundreds.

There is Vonda, intent and focused, and Ed Bryant, before his hair was long enough to rival Rapunzel's; Ted Chiang, quiet and mostly silent, who never missed a word or a nuance. Octavia Butler—so shy, it was hard to induce her to say anything, so shy, I wanted to cuddle her. Instead, we kicked her and told her to write the stories that no one on earth except Octavia Butler could write. Kathe Koja, unaware yet of the potency of her dark, sexual symbolism; Kim Antieau, cool, poised, with her tightly curled toes betraying her anxiety. Kim Stanley Robinson, already deeply serious, and George Alec Effinger, who never was. Forever will he be Piglet in my mind, with his devilish sense of humor and a gleam in his eyes. Lucius Shepherd, a mobile disaster zone; in his presence, things broke, items fell down, drinks spilled. He needed Clarion the way a bulimia victim needs a girdle. All the Mikes with their black beards, five of them one year. Eileen Gunn, world-wise, with a trip around the globe in her past, and Leslie What, trying (and failing) to look mature. Bill Cornet, a tall, gangling redhead, still a teenager, whom the women delighted in teasing because he blushed so readily. Robert Crais, as debonair and handsome then as he still is, and Jim Kelly, who had been too young when he first attempted Clarion. Bravely, he returned another year, and has since become one of the valued instructors. Carol Cooper, rebelling against "white" prose. Laura Mixon, scribbling in her notebook, quite likely writing lyrics for one of her naughty songs. The two Michaelas, Mikey and Mickey. The two Cynthias, master chefs both.... There they all are with their quirks and their charm.

Also present are the ones who will remain nameless: the woman who seduced everything that moved, then apologized to the director because she had run out of time before getting to him. The woman who wielded her knitting needles with a little smile on her face while her stories were being critiqued, and never said a word afterward. The brain surgeon who sold a story, and the attorney with an agenda who didn't. The ex-burglar on crutches; he broke his leg jumping off a roof. The woman whose mother threatened to disown her because she wanted to be a writer. The circus clown. The mathematician who couldn't write a sentence under fifty words with fewer than three subordinate clauses. The teachers, secretaries, a biker, athletes, journalists, artists, musicians, poets...

There is Damon wiggling his long skinny toes in his Birkenstocks, and Cory Doctorow, who is watching, perhaps plotting the story in his head in which someone hears Birkenstock-clad feet walking in a dark hall. Or Damon making paper tents to cover dirty bare feet propped up on a low table. Or marching out to tell the man on the riding mower to go cut grass somewhere else, or to tell people in an adjacent room to turn down the television. Or at the chalkboard illustrating a point with a diagram or chart, decorating a manuscript with caricatures. Drawing a happy face to cheer an apt phrase. Damon, revered and feared, then ten minutes later soaked to the skin by a water gun ambush.

Year by year, the walls recede farther into the shadows

as more chairs are brought in and new family members seat themselves. Their intensity can be intimidating, their determination daunting. Their courage is indisputable.

No non-writer can quite grasp how halting and fearful those first steps to self-revelation can be. Fear of derision, revulsion, rejection, even the fear of self-discovery can pose a monumental barrier. Year after year, we watched emerging writers take those first steps, and we sympathized, then rejoiced when the barrier was overcome. We recognized the courage it took.

I have a terrific respect, admiration, and abiding affection for those gifted students who passed my way briefly, and I take undeserved pride in their accomplishments, knowing all the while that I was a very small part in a wonderful experimental program that worked, and continues to work.

There is always some material that doesn't fit neatly into the five W's—who, where, what, when, and why. We often gave advice, sometimes warnings, about writing in general, and often it was ignored, as happens with most advice. I remember advice I was given as a novice writer; some of it I could use, some I put aside until later, some I never got around to. James Blish advised me to stop writing for a time and go back to read more early science fiction, which I had missed if it was not in library anthologies. I never did. My first novel editor advised me to stay in one genre, mystery fiction, if I wanted to become a successful writer. I couldn't do that either. I was advised on how to write query letters, and they always proved impossible to me. Richard "Mac" McKenna said, "Write only what you want to." I took that to heart. So I know the route most advice takes.

What follows is not a set of rules carved in stone, but just advice from two people who had been there to others who had yet to go.

For instance, your subject matter. It is so individual, so bound up with each writer's personality and private needs that there is no generalizing possible. I like to think that each of us has a niche that no one else can fill, and there's no point in trying to occupy someone else's niche, because there is no room there for more than one. You should write what you are compelled to write, what you feel passionate about, not to please a particular editor, or to fit into a particular market. Editors come and go and markets change, but you will endure for a very long time, and only you can write your material.

Our students often worked furiously to try to keep up with one another in output, in reading, in playing, and frequently they failed. They were trying to work with the wrong rhythm. We reassured them as best we could. If another writer is comfortable writing a story a week, and you cannot do that, don't fret. Take ten days, or two weeks, or whatever your personal schedule requires. Some writers can finish a novel in three months; others need three years, or even longer. They all have their own rhythms. You will find yours. You will deplete your well of inspiration, and in its own time, it will refill and be ready for you to draw on again. There is little point in trying to force it to conform to a faster pace.

Don't worry about style. It matters not at all that X writes poetically and uses phrases that are enviable and you naturally write spare prose. Don't try to force yourself to adopt the style of X. It won't take, and you will only make yourself miserable. Your style develops as you solve your own writing problems because basically that is what style means: it is how each writer solves individual problems of translating nonverbal material into verbal material. It happens and becomes unique to each writer.

Don't worry about getting an agent as long as you are still writing short stories. Agents make 15 percent of what you earn from writing. Literary markets pay little or nothing except contributors' copies of their magazines. Pulp magazines pay a few cents a word. There are very few slick magazines still publishing fiction, and they are inundated with submissions. At one time, *Redbook* was getting 35,000 submissions a year, and they were using no more than two short stories an issue for a total of twenty-four stories a year. The odds are not in a new writer's favor. There are online publications that pay well, or nothing. In any event, selling short fiction is not something that most agents are willing to attempt. Fifteen percent of nothing or 15 percent of a hundred dollars or so is not worth their time and effort.

Use the library to look up anthologies in whatever fields you're interested in: best-of-the-year anthologies in mysteries, science fiction, fantasy, literary fiction, mainstream, whatever. They always list the publications where stories first appeared, and that can be your guide to suitable markets for your own work.

Never engage an agent who charges reading fees, and be wary of story doctors who charge to fix your manuscript. They both make good livings from inexperienced writers.

Marry rich and/or keep your day job.

Don't expect to make a living writing for a long time, if ever. Many successful writers don't make a real living from it after many, many years. Some successful writers never make a living writing fiction.

Be wary of contracts that bind you to future work. I met a young man who had published half a dozen or more novels after leaving Clarion. When I congratulated him on his success, he confided that he had fallen into the contract trap. He had sold his first novel on the basis of an outline and chapters, collected a small advance, and spent it long before the novel was completed. He felt forced to sign a new contract in order to eat while he finished his first novel, and that has been his pattern ever since. He is always working under contract deadlines, writing novels he no longer wants to write, but in need of the next advance.

It would be much better to complete the novel and then, if necessary, sell it on the basis of an outline and chapters. At least the novel is complete before the advance is spent, and you can take time to consider what you want to do next.

Read! I can't stress this enough. We were always amazed at how little many of our students read. Choose books outside your own field of interest: science books, physics, geology, anthropology, archeology, history, ancient history, current events. Read books with views in opposition to your own. You won't remember in detail what you read, but you will have a range of possibilities to explore with your characters. A geologist does not see the same landscape that a fisherman sees; a forester does not see the same woods that an ad agency man sees. If you have gone from K to twelve, then spent four to eight more years in academia and now teach English literature, you won't see the same world as a laborer, who got his first job at eighteen and has worked at hard labor ever since. You can't experience it all, but you can get an inkling through reading.

Keep good records. Keep rejection slips, for instance. If you can prove that you have seriously attempted to write and sell, you can claim a tax deduction for your expenses, but you will need records.

You can't learn how to write a novel by reading a how-to book or two or attending a novel-writing class. The only way to learn to write anything is by writing, including novels. Your first one may become a best seller, or it may never sell, but you will know if you can finish a novel, if you can sustain your interest that long, and you may find the second one easier to write and then to publish.

Be careful whom you ask to read anything if you expect useful feedback. Mom is not the first choice, nor is the dearly beloved other in your life. Either may be quite good, but chances are that is not the case. Non-professionals rarely make good first readers, although they may be astute readers of published work. And non-professionals who love you are even less likely to be good readers for your unpublished work.

After you mail off a story, start a new one just as soon as your own writing rhythm allows. Don't wait for the check to come, or for any other feedback.

If you hit a slump and find you are not writing anything, dig out one of your rejected stories and try rewriting it from a different viewpoint. Sometimes changing from third person to first person lets you see that your characters have been plot-driven instead of acting as rational human beings. You could force your hero to dash into the burning building, but in first person you would not dream of doing such a thing. Or try analyzing the contents by noting in the margin exactly what happens paragraph by paragraph, or do any of the other analytical tricks already suggested. It could be that a slump means only that you have been forcing yourself into an unnatural writing rhythm, or you are signaling yourself that it is time to write something quite different, or there is some other message that you cannot yet decipher and your brain is rebelling, waiting for you to get it.

It frequently happens that a writer is stopped temporarily because he or she has reached a plateau and is getting ready for a new phase, a new kind of writing, or tackling a different kind of material. You may find that on the other side of a slump you are writing very different stories, very likely more complex and deeper than before.

If a slump persists and becomes a real block that goes on for weeks or months, there are a few other things you can try to maneuver yourself out of it.

Try rewriting someone else's stories, first a story you did not particularly like, then one you admired. You could learn something valuable from each, how the one you liked worked its magic, and why the one you did not like was publishable. When I first started to write, after reading a story I thought was bad, what I did was give myself permission to write a bad story by saying I can do that. It's okay to give yourself permission to write a bad story, just as it's okay to admit you were wrong about a story.

Something else you can try in order to break out of a block is to use one of your own characters and do a thorough character study. Write everything you can think of about the character, what he likes for breakfast, where he went to kindergarten, his first girlfriend, his first love affair, everything. Make a house plan for where he lives, and describe the furnishings. You may get so bored, you would rather be writing new material, or you could learn a lot about your characters that you have been missing.

Try the plot outline sketch, starting with a what-if situation problem, one, two, three possible solutions, and then a couple more. Do several of them. You may find that one appeals enough · to you that you want to write the story it suggests.

Gene Wolfe once said that if he got blocked, he would not permit himself to read anything for pleasure, or watch television, listen to music, or go to a movie. He denied himself any mental recreation, and the block never lasted more than a few days.

Try combining elements from two of your stories to create a third one. If one is about space exploration and one about an ancient Egyptian amulet with magical power, combine them and see what happens. Or try the same thing using two totally different dreams.

Write a play.

Joe Haldeman said about a block, It goes away or you die. I don't know of anyone who ever died of writer's block.

Every writer has to discover how much revision is natural and necessary for himself. James Sallis once said that his first draft informed him about what he then would write. Another writer friend claims that her novels come to life in the revision and that she dislikes writing the first draft. For her, the first draft is hard work, but the revision is a pleasure. Robert Heinlein, on the far end of that spectrum, said never rewrite unless directed to do so by your editor. We all fall somewhere in between the two extremes.

I don't like to rewrite and try to keep it to a minimum. I would much rather work and rework scenes mentally before I put a word on paper than to write them and then rewrite them as often as I do in my head. Some writers can become so obsessive about rewriting that they write the life out of a story, or they never leave it and avoid going on to something new since this one is not finished yet.

Many writers feel a compulsion to make their work as perfect as possible as they go, rewriting sentences, or recasting phrases until they are exactly right, and then moving on. As long as they then move on, fine. Just don't get stuck midway through the endless search for perfection.

Sometimes writers would rather never finish a piece of work and risk rejection than finish and submit it and get on with something else. The avoidance devices are many and varied. Continuously rewriting old material can become an avoidance trap. You obviously can't move on until the current work is finished. Looking up words or other details can be used to avoid finishing a piece. If you have a stack of books you must read for just the right detail, obviously you can't move on yet. Stopping one story to start another is a good way to avoid ever finishing. Waiting for feedback or for a check is always good for months. No point in starting something new until you find out if what you're doing is acceptable. Right? Attending seminars, writers' conferences, conventions, even workshops can take up a lot of time and keep you away from work, and since you are making contacts, you can justify using your time that way. Any physical complaint, headache, hangnail, hangover—they all work. Or your printer is acting up, or your computer is behaving oddly. Any of these dodges allows you to call yourself a writer without having to risk actually writing, submitting your work, and subjecting yourself to possible rejection.

Be very careful about having a piece of a novel critiqued. I know some workshops critique novels a chapter at a time, and I warn you that it can be dangerous to the work as a whole. It is a lot like criticizing several lines of the second act of a play; that will tell you nothing about the work as a whole. A novel is a very complicated work of art, with its own rhythms, the ebb and flow of action, subplots, under story, often a slow development of characters, and its own echoes and reverberations throughout. No single piece can inform a reader about the whole. The criticism you get might not fit at all the idea of the novel in your head or in your outline. At most it can point out language problems or syntax, and presumably by the time you are ready to write novels, you will have mastered these tools. Criticism that might work well with a novel the workshop wants to read might be harmful to the one you are actually working on.

When you submit chapters and an outline, the chapters will tell the editor whether there is an enticing opening, one that will make a reader want more. The quality of the writing will be revealed. The outline is little more than information about whether you have enough plot or story to carry a novel full length, and enough about the actual happenings to come to get an idea of where the novel is heading. You don't have to slavishly follow an outline; few editors would expect that.

When an editor tells you that something is not working and makes a suggestion about how to fix it, you have to be the judge of whether that is the right fix. Editors are very happy to have the writer come up with better fixes than theirs. One editor I know says she never suggests how to fix anything, since she is not a writer. She can only say if something is not right and leave it to the writer to make it better.

If an editor tells you a story is too long, that's probably right. The emotional impact and length are bound together, and an experienced editor knows when it's out of proportion. It's usually up to you to figure out how to cut it.

Don't let a bad review get you down, or a good one go to your head. In the end, neither means a lot as long as they spell your name right.

Keep all papers—copyedited manuscripts, editorial notes, reviews, contracts, your own story notes, everything. When you become famous, they will be quite valuable.

Never sign anything you don't understand. There are many writers' organizations that can help with contracts. Get competent advice.

One year at Clarion, I had the students pick up their current stories and hold them at shoulder height. Then I said, "Now let it fall." Papers fluttered to the floor, and students looked at me as if I had lost my mind. I said, "Repeat after me, 'I am not my story.'" They did, and comprehension dawned. You are not your story. It may be rejected time after time, but you are not your story. You have not been rejected even one time. You can let it go. I was told that later that night one could hear papers falling to the floor for a long time.

When you are feeling depressed and it all seems hopeless, go back to the library and consider all those books, all those writers who made it. Find the place where your own books will be shelved, and then go home and get to work.

The Days

During the years that we were shunted from one high-rise building to another, Damon and I walked all over the campus. After we were moved to the Van Hoosen units, we discovered a wooded area behind the buildings, and that became our preferred trail. Our days were full: up at seven thirty, breakfast in our apartment, workshop from nine until twelve, twelve thirty or even later, lunch with the students usually, then a full afternoon of individual conferences with students.

At first, those conferences were for an hour, but we shortened that to fifty minutes, and in the ten-minute intervals between students, we took walks in the woods next to the sluggish brown river. We always invited whoever was with us to come along, but they seldom did, and whether it was because of the mosquitoes, which were mobilized, unionized, and fierce, or because they were too tired or lazy, or more likely because their own workload was also hard, or they needed a little nap time, whatever the reason, we were happy to go by ourselves. Five minutes one way, turn around, and five minutes back, ready for the next conferee. We never insisted or issued the invitation in any way forcefully, although one woman reported back indignantly to the group that we made her walk with us.

We knew they confided in one another about the

conferences; they told us they did. One woman returned to the dorm in tears, wailing that she had no problems. She meant no story problems, of course. Since we had read everything she had done at Clarion when we talked to her, it was not difficult to spot what was holding her back. She has long since gone on to become a very fine, award-winning writer. She searched for and found problems.

The conferences ranged from intense to casual chats. Sometimes Damon or I pulled a past story from the stack to discuss; sometimes the student did, eager for yet another opinion. That our opinions often differed did not matter. The first time it came up in class, that we disagreed on a story, there were shocked looks here and there, but I had warned them that we were not bookends, and an opinion is exactly that, an opinion. We never disagreed on the technicalities of writing, the word usage, sentence structures, and such, but once the objective and correctable issues were done with, what was left was opinion, which is always subjective. So second opinions, third, fourth—they all counted.

I like the lines written by the philosopher Alfred North Whitehead: "Art is the imposition of pattern on experience. Appreciation of art is recognition of the pattern." Sometimes you recognize the pattern and find it agreeable; sometimes you don't. One informed opinion is as valuable as the next.

Many of the students wanted to discuss nothing other than stories, and some wanted to talk about home situations, whether two writers could get along as a couple for more than a few years, if it was too big a gamble to try to make a living as a freelance writer, whatever was on their minds. Some of them approached us in fear and dread, and often confessed that they were terrified that one or the other, or worse, both of us, would say, Forget it, do something else. We never told anyone to give it up. We always insisted that anyone who made it into Clarion had enough talent to become a writer. But we could not judge how much determination and perseverance anyone had. Time would tell. On the other hand, anyone who would give it up on the advice of someone else probably is making the right choice.

One young man said that if he couldn't sell to the highest-paying market, he refused to offer his work to anyone else. He couldn't, and he sank out of sight. He was a very gifted writer, but not even he could start at the top.

Some of the students arrived at Clarion as accomplished writers, but they needed something, if only to be reassured that they were already writing at a professional level.

Although one man had had some success at writing pornography, he had not been able to publish anywhere else. Damon took one of his stories and I took another, and we circled every word that was blatantly pornography or else coded pornography. He was amazed. He had not realized that he had formed habits that he now had to break.

Now and then, someone wanted us to say what kind of stories he or she should write, strive for the literary markets, or the science fiction and fantasy field, or something else. We never advised anyone about what to write, only to write whatever they did as well as possible. In fact, we hated it when a previous instructor gave an assignment to write a story on a particular subject, or handed out a sentence that was to be the opening line of a story, or any other assignment that constricted the writers in any way. One such assignment was to write about labor unions! No one in that group had had any experience whatsoever with labor unions, and correspondingly less interest. Those stories, left for us to critique, were almost always uniformly bad.

After the individual conferences were finished, we had two students back at a time, and Damon and I each walked one through the process of line editing a manuscript. I don't think either of us ever got all the way through a story before time ran out. That was more time consuming, more grueling than the conferences, demanding very close attention, and constant explanations. But it was worth doing, and possibly more valuable than the conferences had been. We wanted to help them learn to look at their own work with the same objectivity that an editor would apply. That is remarkably hard to do for novice and professional writers alike.

And so it went. The conferences were tiring, and when the last one of the day ended, Damon was ready for a nap, and I for a glass of wine. People often dropped in late in the afternoon, and we waited for the new stories to be delivered, and then we usually walked to town to have dinner in a restaurant. Our tolerance for cafeteria food had long since vanished, and we rarely ate there, except for lunch. Our favorite restaurant within walking distance was Mexican, Ramon's, about a mile away. The day would be sweltering, and we were exhausted, but we needed the walk. The dim, cool restaurant, a "marguerita," and good food did wonders of restoration.

We had open house every night from when we returned from dinner until about eleven, for several years; later the curfew became ten o'clock. We needed time to read for the coming day. Time to shower off the mosquito repellent we doused ourselves with every day. Bed, up again at seven thirty, and do it all again.

But Damon's health was deteriorating those last few years. We had to give up our long walks, and then even the shorter ones. David Wright arranged for us to have the use of a university car, and that proved invaluable. Without it, Damon would have had to resign years earlier than he did in spite of his reluctance to do so. But we both knew it was coming before very long.

Things were changing at universities everywhere. The small experimental colleges were being merged into the larger institutions, losing their unique characteristics. MSU was no exception. Justin Morrill College was gone, and after a short period when Michigan State hosted Clarion, Lyman Briggs College became its administrative sponsor. A lack of funding, a perennial problem, threatened Clarion with extinction again. Also there was a question of directorship, if there should be a continuing single director instead of the rotating directors. The pool of possible directors had been shrunken by the deaths of both Lenny Isaacs and Glenn Wright. Others who had served had moved, or were no longer available for one reason or another, and it had become increasingly difficult to find suitable and eligible replacements. The workload for the directors had not diminished over the years; it still involved a great personal sacrifice of time.

In 1993, we thought Damon would make his announcement that his health was forcing him to give it up at the Board of Directors meeting, which was held after the end of the workshop. But we were both uneasy about the possibility that proposals suggested before the board meeting, if accepted, would change the nature of Clarion altogether. One evening we took sandwiches with us to a lake not far from the campus. There, eating our sandwiches, gazing at the placid water with the reflection of a golden sunset riding gently on the surface, Damon said, "One more year."

We had agreed that when the time came, it had to be his decision.

So we went back for one more year, and again and again I caught myself thinking, This is the last time I'll ever do this. It was a saddening thought.

I have mused a lot on what Clarion did and what it meant to the students and teachers alike. Friendships were formed—some of my best friends were first Clarion students, then colleagues, now friends and colleagues. Clarion students formed close ties with one another that endured through decades; they make up a community of respect and affection, support and inspiration, irrespective of distance.

I always felt that some of the students were returning to a sort of literary limbo where they could not find the kind of constructive criticism they might need, and I invited them to send me manuscripts. I reminded them I was not an easy critic, and that my critiques would be very much as they had already experienced. Many of them took me up on the offer, sometimes within months of the most recent workshop, sometimes after several years, even after ten years or longer. I can't guess how many stories, how many first novels I've read over the years. They were always welcome. Damon and I held monthly workshops in our home, and we issued an open invitation to any Clarion student to attend if it was convenient. The workshops continue to this day, and several of the attending members were Clarion students in the seventies, the eighties, up to the current year. Former students keep in touch with notes, holiday cards, family photographs. Some of the early students are now grandparents, and I feel as if I have an extended family of hundreds. It is a good feeling.

When I started to write in the mid- to late 1950s, I did not know a single writer or editor. I had had no instructions, and everything I knew about writing was intuitive. I had no guidelines, and had not come across any helpful books on writing. My first stories were published in science fiction magazines, yet I had never seen such a magazine. I learned later that they were sold in a store that fronted for a bookie, where a sign was posted in the window: NO WOMEN ALLOWED. I never went inside that store. I used an out-of-date market guide, and the names of magazines I culled from library anthologies to try to fathom where to send my own work. Some of the places where I submitted my stories had gone out of business, some had moved, others had changed in significant ways that I knew nothing about. I attended one writers' group meeting at the YMCA at which a woman read poetry intended for a Methodist periodical. A man read a section of a novel he was writing, pornography that embarrassed everyone there. And another woman read a short inspirational vignette that she didn't know where to submit. The group was a mutual admiration society, full of encouragement and praise, and offering nothing useful for me as far as I could tell. The other attendees were as ignorant of the realities of publishing as I was, and I had nothing to offer to any of them. I didn't go back again.

For the first several years of teaching at Clarion, I kept meeting students who had come from the same situation I had been in, isolated, ignorant, unaware of how to prepare a manuscript, how to submit a story, what to say in a query letter, anything to do with professionalism. I kept seeing myself in them. But that began to change after a few years, and the students began coming to the workshop with other workshop experience, with the knowledge of what a manuscript should look like, things that only writers or other professionals in the field usually understand.

What was happening was a phenomenon that seems unique to the field of science fiction and fantasy. At least, I have never found it to the same extent in any other group of writers.

Former students returned to the real world with a dedication to writing that seemed to compel them to share their own experience, share what they had learned, and they organized mini workshops all over the country. They met for an evening, sometimes for a weekend, a full week of critiquing one another's work; they formed workshops at conventions, planned annual intensive workshops, all on a volunteer basis. Some former students became writing teachers at every level of education.

Some have returned to Clarion as instructors; they offer great insight with their understanding of what the students are going through, as well as their own publishing successes. They all use the methods they learned at Clarion, what has come to be called the Milford/Clarion method of honest and supportive criticism with the most knowledgeable writer acting as leader.

Of course, not all those small workshops are being run by people who attended Clarion, but I believe they started what has become a continuing trend, and they inspired others to do the same. Now it is doubtful if there is an aspiring writer who does not have such a workshop within a reasonable distance. The isolation, frustration, and bewilderment many of us felt when we began to write are no longer necessary prerequisites for a career in publishing.

I have often said I learned everything I know about writing at Clarion. The students are teachers of the teachers. From starting as intuitive writers to becoming analytical critics is a major step for many of us, and participating in a demanding workshop hones that skill in ways that are immeasurable. To be forced to analyze and then explain any creative process is in itself an education. Many of the students came to realize that hearing a wide range of opinions and being compelled to think through and express their own opinions was of equal or even greater value than having their own work critiqued. Students make the best teachers.

No one person with the exception of Robin Scott Wilson can take credit for the success of Clarion. It is a gestalt that works as a whole. It cannot even be stated with certainty that those who went on to become successful writers, editors, teachers, critics, script writers would not have done so without the benefit of that summer boot camp. There was no control group. But the stacks of manuscripts in the slush piles are still towering, and perhaps they serve as a comparison. And the testimony of those who did attend is positive. Many of them feel that attending Clarion made a significant difference in their lives, made their future success possible.

As I write, there is yet another funding crisis, that recurring nightmare that has besieged Clarion intermittently from its beginning. Yet Clarion is an entity in and of itself. Michigan State University has been a superb host for Clarion, and Lyman Briggs College, its administrative sponsor, has been unfailingly supportive, yet Clarion is not an official part of either. It is a separate entity, one that set its own rules and lived by them throughout the years. It is not an official summer workshop of the university even though university credits are available. Whether it will survive the current crisis is not determined at this date, but even if it is not funded under the present economic crisis that faces most states and most educational institutions, I am confident that it will survive in some other way. It fills a need that no other workshops, no other creative writing program fills. Its influence extends throughout the world of contemporary literature.

» **Notes and Lessons on Writing**

These notes and lessons are drawn from the previous chapters. They are intended to serve as a series of pointers, reminders, and refreshers for writers of all levels on the basics of writing, and will help in avoiding some of the most common mistakes.

Following these notes are a few practical writing exercises also drawn from the book.

» The Elements of Story

Where to Begin?

Openings are hard, and they are the only showcase most beginning writers get. At Clarion, Damon and I never had to wait longer than the first day for a story to provide more than enough material to discuss openings.

The opening *has* to work because no matter how good the story might turn out to be, if no one reads beyond the first page, the story will not be published. Most often the showcase is no longer than these two paragraphs.

No one glancing through a stack of stories is going to analyze the openings, but if the sense of insecurity is strong because of many unanswered questions, awkward phrases, or misused words, if there is no compelling reason to turn the page, that story has had its chance, and the reader moves onto the next one.

So, when beginning a story, do not:

· Let your viewpoint meander.
· Confuse immediate setting with background and let your camera eye wander in, out, and about randomly.
· Start with a lecture in anything—history, physics, biology—*anything*. Expository lumps anywhere are to be avoided if possible, but they are deadly in the opening.
· Start in the middle of a scene. This is why flashback openings are a mistake almost every time. You interrupt an ongoing scene to tell us something that happened earlier that results in the ongoing scene. Once started, the scenes should be concluded before you move on. An ongoing conversation is hard to catch up with. Who are these speakers, what is their relationship, what kind of voice should I be hearing in my head? Introduce them before they open their mouths.
· Mislead the reader with false information or try to create suspense or arouse curiosity by withholding necessary information. What you arouse is distrust and annoyance.
· Sprinkle around neologisms or made-up words that cannot be found in a dictionary.
· Use words that only you and a few other people in your specialty can understand.
· Use contractions if you can avoid them, and only sparingly no matter what.
· Have your character look into a mirror or other reflective surface in order to work in a description of her.
· Let your character talk to an inanimate object or animal in order to give information to the reader about what is going on.
· Play games with the sex of your character.

Remember the Basics
The basic five W's of journalism (Who? Where? What? When?

Why?) apply equally to writing fiction. They have to be given, or implied, and the sooner the better. Especially the *who* question. Seventh-grade teachers stress the need to start with a dramatic scene to capture the attention of a (seventh-grade) reader. Consequently there are a lot of stories that start with bullets whizzing over someone's head, or someone running for his life, or a different dramatic situation equally empty.

If a story starts with the most powerful image, or the most dramatic scene, it has only one direction it can take: down. Instead, the story should develop naturally to that moment of greatest interest.

Characters: Making Them Real

Where was your character a year before the story began? A month before? Supposing she survives at the end, where will she be tomorrow? Characters shouldn't be born on page one and vanish when the story ends. Even people who discover characters as they write them discover much about their pasts and possible futures.

Today, great fiction is most often written about people who at a glance would appear to be regular, everyday, common folks— like most writers. These ordinary people might become involved in extraordinary adventures, but they remain recognizable as the kind of people you might see on buses, trains, in the subway, in offices, in your own home. Great fiction reveals that there is no such thing as a common, everyday uninteresting person. They are all interesting if you learn enough about them to discover who lives behind the facade. You have to peel away the public layers and find who exists under the skin; then you'll have a realistic character.

As your characters become more obsessed, they often become more interesting. Most readers are fascinated by obsessed characters.

Know the hidden self *and* the public self of your character. Put that character in a real place, and then get on with the story. It sounds so simple: one, two, three. For many inexperienced writers, it proves to be quite elusive and difficult.

Characters: Curiosity

Every living creature shares the trait of curiosity, and the higher the level of intelligence and imagination, the greater the curiosity, until in humans it becomes a powerful drive. We have to know what lies beyond the wall, what treasures or terrors exist in the deepest sea trenches, what is under the frozen poles, what is at the edge of the ocean, over the mountain, in the darkest forests. What is on the dark side of the moon, on Mars, beyond Jupiter? We are driven to learn what is out there.

Setting: World

Think of a story as existing at the peak of a high pyramid, with the foundation anchored in bedrock in a real world. A world exists in which the pyramid is appropriate. Its base is the general setting for the story, and the peak is the immediate setting where the actions of the story take place. They are all necessary. Although the peak is the focus of a short story, the foundation and the world have to be implied one way or another. The immediate setting cannot float in a void.

Setting, world, and culture are so intricately wed to character that it is nearly impossible to talk about one without the other. We are affected by our world and our setting, and we have an effect, however infinitesimal, on it.

Setting: Place

I usually draw house plans for the buildings I write about. I need to know where the doors are, where the halls are, and where they lead to. I often use real city or county maps and alter them to suit my own purposes. Or I draw my own. I need to know how long it would take to get from here to there, what kind of terrain lies between point A and point B. Also, I feel very free to clear an entire area and build my own community, my own woods or city streets, with the kinds of buildings, shops, or whatever else my story needs. I may use a real highway, a street on a city map, and then add another one that isn't on the map. I make that street I just invented as real as possible in my fictional world, and unless you look for it and fail to find it, not only should you never know it is my invention, you should never even ask.

Other writers clear the space also and refurnish it, and that's one of the reasons why you can't use anyone else's fiction for your own research in any way. A published writer may have a hundred or more details of the setting to work with—some inventions, others based on the real world. She can pick and choose from a wealth of information what she needs, and end up using no more than ten details. If you use that writer's details for your own setting, you start with ten to pick from, and since you can't use them all or you could be guilty of plagiarism, you might end up using one or two details, and the ones you choose could well be the invention of the original writer. One setting will be rich and plausible; the second one will be flat and unconvincing.

The city I see is not the same one you might see. One who knows plants can go into the country and return with a basket of edible greens where someone else sees only unkempt weeds. We all have different areas of interest, a different focus even when we're looking at the same landscape, or at the same person.

You must do whatever research is necessary for your story, and primary sources are always the first choice. If you are writing about a museum, visit a few, pay attention to the lighting, the placement of art, and so on. Read up on museums. With the

Internet available to almost everyone, research has become so accessible that there is no excuse for anyone not to make use of it. Fiction should never be a primary source for your research. Whatever that published writer learned has been filtered through that writer's needs, which are never your needs. What works well is to use enough of what's real to establish a solid core of belief, and then invent as you need to.

Setting: The Imaginary

Beginning science fiction or fantasy writers sometimes argue that because theirs is a work of pure imagination, they are free to invent whatever they want. I agree, but your world has to be consistent to make it plausible. If you are writing about an immense Saharan desert with nothing but sand dunes from horizon to horizon, you can't plant a tree to provide convenient shade.

Whatever setting you use, make sure it is consistent within itself and with whatever period you are writing about. If you know what lies on the other side of the wall, enough of that information will infiltrate the story so that we, the readers, will believe in the reality of your world.

Plot: Situation and Event

I think of the situation as the precipitating event. There is order, equilibrium, and no matter how chaotic or dangerous life is, if that's the status quo, that's the equilibrium. A fireman risking his life, a soldier going into battle, a deep-sea explorer going down in a submersible—if it is his job, something he does routinely, that's the equilibrium. Something upsets it, and it must be resolved. That "something" is the precipitating event, and now you have a situation to be developed.

One way the situation can be made into story is to develop it laterally. There is visible cause and effect. The hero acts, and there is an effect—good or bad—and he acts again, then again, until by the end of the story, you have restored equilibrium or order.

Or it can be developed vertically. No one does much possibly, there may be no visible cause and effect, but the situation is explored in more and more depth, its implications explored, and by the end the reader has been informed of the true meaning of the situation and what it means to the characters. At the end of this kind of story, the situation may be exactly as it was in the beginning, and what has changed is the reader's understanding. This story may be quiet and introspective, or it may be very active with a lot of adventures, confrontations, but the action does not have an effect on the basic situation.

Quite often a story seems to lie midway between the two methods. The situation is developed thoroughly, but the protagonist does not act until the end of the story and you have no way of knowing exactly what that action will mean in the future. That is just another kind of plotted story with most of the real plot implied, or left to the reader to supply. The situation is changed because finally the character is going to do something about it, but the only effect is by implication.

All the approaches above are valid; no one is better than another morally, ethically or esthetically. They all can and do produce very good fiction, or quite bad fiction. You may prefer one to another as a writer or a reader, and that's valid also. What is not valid is to say, I didn't understand this story, or I don't like this kind of story; therefore, it's a bad story. Tastes in fiction vary as much as in any other area, as they should.

Plot Loops: Something to Avoid
Plot loops are deadly for a story. A woman wrote a story about a husband-and-wife team of researchers who had made

a momentous discovery, and were in the middle of an intense struggle about whether to release it. Ethical problems were apparent, and they were in a bind. Then the man goes off to a family gathering and for three or four pages he is surrounded by a whole new set of characters who have nothing to do with the story. He returns and picks up the struggle where it left off. That is a typical plot loop. Plot loops can always be snipped right out and never missed.

Plot: Choices That Matter
The characters can't just do what they normally do or make choices that don't make any difference. They have to do things they do not want to do or make hard choices. If the decision matters little to the character, if it is a choice of accepting good fortune or not, if it is a victory without a fight, it will not matter to a reader.

In the classic movie *Butch Cassidy and the Sundance Kid,* Butch and the Kid are running from a relentless posse. They try every trick and stratagem they know but can't elude them. The outlaws reach a cliff high over a river, and now their choices are to give up, or shoot it out and die. Unexpectedly, and delightfully, a third choice presents itself. They can jump into the river far below. It is a terrible choice, but over they go. That unexpected third option is always a wonder, always a delight to the reader.

That was an action adventure film, and you wouldn't introduce anything that extreme into a domestic story. But people have to make difficult choices all the time. There are always options, possible ways out of a dilemma, but each option comes with a price tag, either financial or emotional.

Plot: Considering the Alternatives
One of the reasons that most teachers in middle school through

high school and into college courses and, regrettably, even intensive workshops teach plotting as the major storytelling method is that it is teachable, and it is learnable. There is a template, and no matter how much the story parts are scrambled in the words on paper, if the story is restored to a chronological timeline, the pattern is discernible. Parts may be skimped, or even missing, but the story follows certain guidelines; it moves from order to disorder and back to order.

Paradoxically, many (perhaps even most) very short stories do not follow that template. It is hard to fit a real plot into a story under five thousand words, but even more important, much short fiction is not about overcoming obstacles. It is about how people behave, who they are, how they fit into society, how technology influences their lives, how they manage or mismanage their relationships, things of personal interest.

By its nature, the unplotted story exists in a state of anarchy. There are no defining guidelines, no templates, no rules to follow—only general broad principles. It is easy enough to critique such stories on the basis of success or failure, but even that is highly subjective. You dig it or you don't.

Having said that, I can give a hint of the principles. If it is a day-in-the-life-of story, the life being illuminated must be thoroughly plumbed and understood, and its essence presented in the story. Whether it's the life of a barefoot peasant or a society trendsetter, that life must be understood and explored and meaning derived from it. The peasant may have a life that a sophisticated city dweller would find intolerable, but by the end of the peasant's story, she should have an understanding that she never had before about him or his life. And, of course, the writer can't reveal the meaning of this life unless and until she has thoroughly grasped it.

» The Forms

The Short Story

A short story is a narrative work of fiction under an arbitrary length that is variable depending on who is counting and for what purposes. A *successful* short story is a marvel of compression, nuance, inference, and suggestion. If the novel invites one to enter another world, the short story invites one to peer through a peephole into the world, and yet the world has to have the same reality as in a novel. It truly is the universe in a grain of sand. This is done by compression and implication. Every single word has to help the story, or it hurts it. The short story is the least forgiving form of narrative fiction. There is no room for redundancies, for backing up to explain what was meant before, for authorial intrusions that may be perfectly allowable in the novel.

This is one reason why the flashback, useful in novels, is usually a mistake in the short story. There is not enough space allowed to go over the same territory twice. Those writers who apply novelistic techniques to the short story invariably fail.

In the short story, there must be the moment of truth where something important to the characters is at stake; or there has to be a moment of truth in which the reader comes to realize what is at stake even if the characters remain oblivious. *Someone* has to react to the moment of truth of the story.

The Novelette

A novelette is more restricted, usually has one main character, and a story line that is followed with few diversions. The form allows for room to explore a small part of the world, but that part may be well developed.

The Novella

A novella usually has one main thoroughly developed story line, with minor subplots often hinted at rather than explicated. The novel opens a world; the novella opens a piece of it. Hemingway's *The Old Man and the Sea* is a good example. Also, the novella allows for several characters who weave in and out of the main story line with their own viewpoints.

The Novel

A novel opens a door into another world and invites the reader to enter and explore it with the writer. Whether the other world is on a different planet, in a different period of time, or is placed here and now, it is always a different world.

In the novel, plots and subplots—and usually many characters—are developed, and often many viewpoints are used. There is no time or space restriction; the writer is free to wander through the past, the present, the future, and roam the entire universe. A novel is a forgiving form of fiction and for many reasons, excluding length, the easiest to write.

Note: for the genre-writing awards, short stories are 7,500 words and under. A novelette is from 7,500 words to about 15,000. A novella is from 15,000 to 40,000 words, and a novel is 40,000 words and up.

» The Writing Life

Taking the Time

No one gives writing time to a new writer, or in many cases to an established writer. Each and every one of us has to take it, forcibly if necessary, by wile, bribery, any method that works. You have to take the time, to weigh it against whatever else is happening, to give it up somewhere else, sacrifice time with other people, time for movies, time for television, fun, games, partying, sleep, or something. There is always some time every day to set aside and declare one's own, but it requires a lot of self-discipline to seize it and keep it. If not every day, then three days a week, and if that's still impossible, one day a week.

It's hard in the beginning because there is no payback or tangible reward for all that time spent alone in thought or at a keyboard, and life keeps getting in the way. But it is absolutely necessary to find the time and keep it inviolable and recognized by the private world of the writer that it is not to be invaded.

Paradoxically, and cruelly, the ones you love the most and who love you are the greatest problem. They see you suffering, alone, withdrawn, apparently getting nowhere, and they want to help. Something is offered, and if you say no, feelings get hurt, guilt arises.

You have to decide which guilt to live with: the guilt of denying the companionship or the guilt of yielding and not writing or working at an aspect of writing.

Emotional Sources

By the time a child is eight to ten years old, he or she has experienced every possible human emotion. Those childhood slings and arrows provide the bottomless well to draw upon for your characters.

Face your emotions. Acknowledge them and examine them. Then use them.

The Self

It is a truism that a writer reveals the self, sometimes in full awareness, sometimes unconsciously, but that is the goal. That finally is all that any of us has to offer as writers: our own perceptions of the world, our own interpretation of our culture, our experiences in fictional terms. Just as a writer must be a people watcher, the writer must look inward for the emotion that drives people. Watch people to see the range of behavior; look inward to find the cause.

Think of the worst incident of your life, and use it. Change all the objective details, make the character the opposite sex, older or younger, in a completely different situation, but keep the emotional truth. Do it again with your happiest day. You are plumbing the depths of yourself, and of truth.

Take Criticism…

Beginning writers need more than just encouragement in the form of pats and praise. Many have been writing and submitting stories for years without any tangible encouragement from beyond their own circle of admirers. They need to know *why* they are not succeeding. A workshop like Clarion is where they can find out. It is hard and it is demanding, and for those who understand and accept what it can do, it is a shortcut, often of many years.

Writers can get pats and praises from their mothers, lovers, and spouses. What they can get at Clarion are honest evaluations of their work from professionals who know what is publishable and what isn't most of the time, and who can offer advice that the home folk are not trained to give. Yes, it is hard and demanding. No one ever said it would be easy.

…But Don't Get Discouraged!

When you are feeling particularly low and depressed, go to the library. All those books were written by individuals who started at the bottom: rejected, unwanted, unloved, too depressed to continue at times, and yet … there they are, there are the works they produced, their books loved by many, read, reread, preserved through the years. Sit down and let yourself feel the presence of all those writers who also struggled, and who persevered and whose works live on.

» Points to Keep in Mind

· It is not an editor's job to teach craft to a beginning writer.
· If you can describe your character with a two- or three-word phrase, you're probably writing a stereotype.
· Pay attention to the differences in the way men and women talk.
· Fiction is first and foremost about people—even big ideas are secondary. This is often disputed in the world of science fiction, but nowhere else that I know.
· It's a good practice to know who the person is before you know what the person does.
· Stories told by a detached observer can rarely arouse suspense or create tension in the reader who wants the vicarious experience of someone living through the events.

» Short Fiction Conventions

· The first named character is the one the story is about.
· The character has to be qualified to do whatever is required in the story.
· We have to know what the limits are.
· Beginning writers often confuse predictability with inevitability.
· *Deus ex machina* is a useful phrase to remember: It never works to have a new character solve the hero's problem, or have fate step in, or a miracle, or God. If it is John's problem, let him deal with it.
· Killing off characters does not add suspense to stories.
· A threat has to be real, and it has to put the character in jeopardy.

- As James Blish put it: Don't call a rabbit a *smeerp*.
- A plotted story consists of a situation that is problematic. There are attempts to alleviate it or get rid of it altogether, which usually fail or make it worse. There is a crisis where all seems lost. Then there is the final solution that resolves the problem and changes the situation.
- A literary or academic approach to story is not the same as a writer's analytical approach.
- Symbols are so intimately bound to the writer's personal experiences and style that to draw attention to them might cause the writer to become self-conscious, and even to try to impose symbols, instead of letting them emerge naturally.
- *Some* things about writing can be taught. Anyone with fair talent, a great deal of determination and perseverance, and some luck, can become a publishable writer.
- For many writers, no story is ever truly finished; at some point it is abandoned. It is important to learn which abandoned story should be submitted for possible publication, and which ones should be put away.

» Useful Chapters to Refer Back To:

» Writing Exercises

Sentences

Using a finished story, take clean paper and cover everything but one sentence. Read that sentence. Does it say exactly what you intended and nothing else? That's it.

For example: "'Don't do that!' he exploded."

Looks okay? Wrong. You can't explode words. You can utter them, say them, mutter, murmur, yell, shout, whisper, and so on.

De-purpling

Purple prose is prose in which the modifiers—adjectives and adverbs usually—overwhelm the nouns and verbs.

Take them out. Each and every one of them. Not just the immediate modifiers, but also the modifiers of the modifiers.

For example: "The full, ballooning moon, glowing as if alive with white-hot fires forged in an unworldly icy hell, rose serenely with its majestically imperial presence over the harsh, frozen, and hostile tundra."

Three or four sentences like that in a row can make the reader lose the story line altogether. Sensory overload sets in with too many images, too many contrasting and competing ideas.

Where is the focus of that sentence? What does it actually say and mean?

The moon rose. Okay, but you might need a little more than that.

After you strip the entire story down to its bare bones, start at the beginning and see just how many of the modifiers you must restore. *The full moon rose over the frozen tundra.* If that is what you need to convey, stop there.

Sensory overload can be more deadly to a story than minimalist prose. You may be surprised to find a much stronger story than you started with once it's relieved of its overwhelming finery.

If most of your verbs are paired with adverbs, use stronger verbs. They should not need crutches.

Paragraphs
Your story is as flawless as you can make it, and yet is unpublishable. One way to find out why is to examine it with a different set of tools.

Start with the first paragraph, read just that paragraph several times and then write in the margin what happens in it or what it is about. You may decide it's a description of the place, the setting. Write *setting*. Next paragraph, do the same thing. More setting? Do the next and next.

You may find that by the end of the story you have written *setting* over and over. Or perhaps it was character description, or something else repeated time after time. The story is static, giving the reader more and more of the same thing glossed with beautiful language. Or maybe there is a character moving through the setting. Same diagnosis: a static story, nothing happens.

Dialogue
Write a page or two of dialogue without any attributions. No *he said*, or *she said*, no names, only the dialogue. Your characters' speech patterns should vary enough to distinguish who is speaking, and speech should never sound like the narrative.

Viewpoints

Unless there is a good dramatic reason to describe the characters, try to let the characters within the story see one another according to their own emotional involvement.

A woman enters a restaurant where she is meeting her lover. He is passionately in love with her. Have him describe her. Have someone else present describe her, someone who hates her. Then write a third description made by someone present who is totally neutral. They should not all see the same woman the same way.

Using one of your own stories, write a scene that is confrontational with three people involved. It can be a scene actually written already, or one that will never be used, just use your own characters. First write it from the viewpoint of your protagonist. Then again from the other two viewpoints. Try to visualize your story scenes like this and see if they change. What one person sees as reasonable behavior another might see as belligerent or hostile, or possibly insane.

The Third Resolution

First write a sketch of a situation or outline an idea for a plotted story, and a possible resolution. The next step is to put aside the solution and find another one, a bit more difficult or complicated than the first. Then put that resolution aside, too, and come up with a third one.

If you succeed, you may find the third resolution is one that the reader would not have expected or furnished herself.

Mother Goose

Try telling stories to children. Don't retell stories from books; make them up. Children are a demanding audience. They insist on an identifiable situation, a problem, a solution to the problem, and a satisfying, identifiable resolution. You have to get little

Timmy out of the well, get the robbers out of the house, find the secret door and escape. And you have to do it in a way that your audience would not have thought of. Surprise them. If you can hold a child's attention, you can plot a story.

Kate Wilhelm, born in 1928, is the author of more than thirty novels. Her work has been adapted for TV and film and translated into twenty languages. She has been awarded the Prix Apollo, Kurd Lasswitz, Hugo, Nebula, and Locus Awards. In 2003, she was inducted into the Science Fiction Hall of Fame. Her short fiction appeared in landmark anthologies such as *Again Dangerous Visions, Orbit, The Penguin Book of Modern Fantasy by Women,* and *The Norton Book of Science Fiction.*

A cofounder of the Clarion Writers' Workhops, she continues to host monthly writing workshops in Eugene, Oregon.

Small Beer Press

JOHN CROWLEY, *Endless Things* (978-1-931520-22-5) $24

ALAN DeNIRO, *Skinny Dipping in the Lake of the Dead* (978-1-931520-17-1) $16

CAROL EMSHWILLER
    The Mount ("Best of the Year"—*Book Magazine, Locus, San Francisco Chronicle*) (978-1-931520-03-4) $16
    Report to the Men's Club ("Daring, eccentric."—*Kirkus Reviews*) (978-1-931520-02-7) $16
    Carmen Dog ("A wise and funny book.—*New York Times*) (978-1-931520-08-9) $14

ANGÉLICA GORODISCHER, *Kalpa Imperial* (★ "Dreamy."—*Library Journal*) (978-1-931520-05-8) $16
    TRANSLATED BY URSULA K. LE GUIN

ELIZABETH HAND, *Generation Loss* (978-1-931520-21-8) $24

ELLEN KUSHNER, *The Privilege of the Sword* (978-1-931520-20-1) $35

KELLY LINK
    Magic for Beginners (*Time Magazine* Book of the Year) (978-1-931520-15-7) $24
    Stranger Things Happen (*Village Voice* Favorite · Salon Book of the Year) (978-1-931520-00-3) $16
    Trampoline: an anthology (Editor) (978-1-931520-04-1) $17

LAURIE J. MARKS, *Water Logic* (978-1-931520-23-2) $16

MAUREEN F. McHUGH, *Mothers & Other Monsters* (978-1-931520-19-5) $16

NAOMI MITCHISON, *Travel Light* ("Read it now!"—Ursula K. Le Guin) (978-1-931520-14-0) $12

DELIA SHERMAN & THEODORA GOSS, *Interfictions* (978-1-931520-14-0) $18

JENNIFER STEVENSON, *Trash Sex Magic* ("Absolutely rocks."—Audrey Niffenegger) (978-1-931520-12-6) $16

SEAN STEWART
    Perfect Circle (★ "All-around terrific."—*Booklist*) (978-1-931520-11-9) $15
    Mockingbird (A *New York Times* Notable Book.) (978-1-931520-09-6) $14

HOWARD WALDROP, *Howard Who?* (978-1-931520-18-8) $14

KATE WILHELM, *Storyteller* (978-1-931520-16-4) $16

RAY VUKCEVICH, *Meet Me in the Moon Room* (978-1-931520-01-0) $16

Lady Churchill's Rosebud Wristlet
    A twice-yearly fiction &c zine ("Tiny, but celebrated"—*The Washington Post*) edited by Kelly Link and Gavin J. Grant publishing writers such as Carol Emshwiller, Karen Joy Fowler, Jeffrey Ford, Eliot Fintushel, James Sallis, Molly Gloss, and many others. Fiction & nonfiction from *LCRW* have been reprinted in *The Year's Best Fantasy & Horror, The Best of the Rest,* and *The Zine Yearbook.* Many subscription options (including chocolate) available on our website. *The Best of LCRW* (9780345499134 · $14.95) is also available from Del Rey.

www.smallbeerpress.com